Heinemann EXPLORE Science

Teacher's Book
New International Edition

Grade 1

Tara Lievesley, Deborah Herridge
Series editor: John Stringer

PEARSON

Pearson Education Limited is a company incorporated in England and Wales having its registered office at Edinburgh Gate, Harlow, Essex, CM20 2JE.

Registered company number: 872828

www.pearsonglobalschools.com

Text © Pearson Education Limited 2012
First published 2003. This edition published 2012.

16 15 14 13 12
IMP 10 9 8 7 6 5 4 3 2 1

British Library Cataloguing in Publication Data
A catalogue record for this book is available from the British Library

ISBN 978 0 435133 62 7

Edited by Anna Woodford and Janice Curry
Designed by Techset Ltd, Gateshead
Original illustrations © Pearson Education Limited, 2003, 2009, 2012
Cover photo/illustration © Alamy Images
Printed in China (SWTC/01)

Acknowledgements
Every effort has been made to contact copyright holders of material reproduced in this book. Any omissions will be rectified in subsequent printings if notice is given to the publishers.

New International Edition

Introduction

Heinemann Explore Science New International Edition provides a comprehensive, easy-to-use resource written especially for the international primary classroom.

The teaching framework follows the Cambridge International Examinations Primary Science Curriculum Framework (2011), enabling you to minimize planning. The simple structure of *Heinemann Explore Science* gives you flexibility to teach the Units within a grade in the order that suits your situation.

There is one Unit for each half of a term, the final half term being for assessment and review. There are nine or ten lessons in each Unit. The first lesson in each Unit is an introduction Unit and the last one is a plenary. The other lessons either focus on knowledge and understanding or on manageable, tried and tested investigation activities. The greater the opportunity for investigation, the more practical lessons there are.

Each Grade of *Heinemann Explore Science* contains these detailed teacher's notes in the *Teacher's Book*, providing all the resources you need for planning and teaching successful science lessons; an accompanying *Student Book* to bring the science topics to life for the children; a *Workbook* with activities to do at school or at home, and six *Readers* to develop students' English language skills through science. Alongside these components, digital resources available via online subscription provide an e-book version of the printed books, opportunities for independent research into the Biology, Chemistry and Physics covered in the scheme and further activities and simulations. For more information on digital resources for this course, visit www.pearsonglobalschools.com/explorescience.

This unique combination of science and ICT stimulates students and enables you to deliver enriching science lessons using today's technology.

Heinemann Explore Science and English language development

Science and language development have much in common. In both, students are frequently highly motivated. Science is a popular subject area in primary schools with students (and with teachers!), and produces interesting and engaging results. Language and science are both social activities. Students' language will not develop without co-operation and collaboration, and science is also a collaborative subject. Finally, science experiences can lead, as few other subjects do, to a desire to communicate discoveries.

When developing spoken English, remember:

- Discussion can be stimulated by working in threes. Two friends doing science may have a common and familiar way of communicating. Three extends the discussion.
- Snowball or jigsaw activities, in which groups share and exchange information, are engaging.
- Discussion before and after an investigation can clarify thoughts. Having to explain what students discovered in their investigation helps clarify thinking and improve language skills.
- Presenting results to others imposes a discipline as well as giving purpose to recording and to clear presentation.
- Reading can be developed through following instructions – including safety instructions – and using the *Student* and targeted *Readers*.

Students may be understandably reluctant to record their discoveries. When encouraging written recording, use a variety of recording methods.

- Writing to a structure helps to order students' thoughts.
- Annotated diagrams are an effective way of recording practical science – used by adult scientists as well as students.
- A recorded observation alone may lead to a conclusion.
- Ordering and recording whole investigations is difficult, and can often be better done to a writing framework.

Heinemann Explore Science offers and defines new vocabulary. If the words are new to you, or you have any doubts yourself about their definition, use the definitions in the glossary in the *Student Book*.

- Draw the students' attention to the new words.
- Depending on the students' age, set them to illustrate or define the words themselves. Introduce word games – matching the word to the definition.
- Make a 'Words of Science' poster or a class dictionary.
- Ask the students to use the words in context; to act them out; to guess which word you are thinking of, either by 20 questions or by giving clues.
- Use cloze procedure to place new words.

Components of the scheme

The **Heinemann Explore Science** *Teacher's Book* provides detailed guidance on teaching with the corresponding sections of the *Student Book* pages. Used alongside the electronic components, where you will find a variety of resources for planning and teaching, the *Teacher's Book* is the main starting point for any lesson. Each Unit provides approximately a half-term's worth of work – an introduction, and seven or eight lesson plans (each of which may be taught in a single session or across science sessions during the week), and a final review.

Each Unit introduction provides:

1 Clear background science information to support the non-specialist teacher.

2 Simple definitions of necessary scientific vocabulary.

3 A complete list of resources needed in the Unit.

4 Helpful hints on prior preparation or useful additional resources.

5 Indications of what students should already know and be able to do before starting the Unit.

6 Cross-curricular references to other subject areas.

7 A discussion question to set the scene and introduce a context for the Unit.

There are two types of lesson in **Heinemann Explore Science**. The first type focuses on knowledge and understanding objectives. These lessons contain:

1 Starter activities to initiate whole-class discussion. Questioning will enable you to establish what the students already know.

2 References to the corresponding *Student Book* pages and further information to expand on the paragraphs in the *Student Book*.

3 Safety tips to advise of specific hazards where appropriate.

4 Additional information necessary for the activities in the 'Things to do' section of the *Student Book*, plus suggestions of how to differentiate and record. Any worksheets required are cross-referenced.

5 Integrated ICT research activities using the website.

6 Further details or extra 'fun facts' to support those listed in the *Student Book*.

7 The answer to the 'I wonder ...' question, with additional background explanation if necessary.

8 More activities that can be used instead of, or as well as, those in the 'Things to do' section.

9 Ideas for how students could present their work or tips for classroom displays, including referenced PowerPoint templates, provided on the website to help students.

10 An activity or series of questions to reinforce the main objectives in the plenary session, drawing the lesson to a close.

The second type of lesson offers a challenge to encourage students to use scientific enquiry skills to investigate a problem in context. These contain:

1 Starter activities to initiate whole-class discussion.

2 A challenge introduced in context, explaining what students will be investigating.

3 Safety tips advising of unique hazards where appropriate; an individual risk assessment is always recommended.

4 Further details of how to carry out the investigation, supporting the instructions in the *Student Book*.

5 Lists of materials students will need, including any to be prepared in advance.

6 Explanations of what students should be looking for, or how to keep the test fair. How best to support and extend students.

7 How to organize, record, analyse and present data collected in the investigation. Suitable tables for data recording are provided as worksheets in the *Workbook*.

8 Students are encouraged to review how well they carried out their investigation and how good their results were. Using the report provided for each investigation helps students build evaluation skills by criticizing methods and conclusions.

9 A different scenario is offered to enable students to apply what they have learned.

10 Suggestions for homework activities.

2

11 An activity or series of questions to reinforce the main objectives in the plenary session, drawing the lesson to a close.

At the end of each Unit, material is provided for an assessment and review lesson:

1 A clear summary of the knowledge and skills students have gained through the Unit, divided into three levels of attainment.

2 Explanation and expected responses to the 'Check-up' in the *Student Book*.

3 Answers to the assessment worksheets in the *Workbook*.

4 The answer to the original question posed at the beginning of the Unit.

5 A final activity completes the Unit and reminds students of everything they have learned.

In addition, there are six readers for each Grade of the Framework. These are written to match the appropriate science for the Grade, but with close attention to language levels. Students can learn English language through science, and science through practising their English.

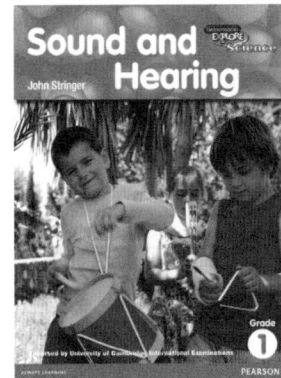

New International Edition

Quick guide to the Teacher's Book

The *Heinemann Explore Science 1* *Teacher's Book* provides detailed guidance on teaching with the corresponding sections of the *Student Book* pages. Used alongside the e-book, where you will find a variety of resources for planning and teaching, the *Teacher's Book* is the main starting point for any lesson. Each Unit provides approximately one half-term's worth of work and comprises an introduction and generally six or seven lessons (each of which may be taught all at once, or across a number of science sessions during the week), plus a review.

Each Unit introduction provides:

2 A complete list of resources needed throughout the Unit.

3 Indicators of what students should know and be able to do before starting this Unit.

1 Clear background science information to support the non-specialist teacher.

4 Specific references to other subject areas.

7 Useful definitions of scientific vocabulary commonly misunderstood by students.

6 Helpful hints on prior preparation or useful resources.

5 An initial discussion question to set the scene and introduce a context for the Unit.

There are two types of lesson in *Heinemann Explore Science*. The first type focuses on knowledge and understanding objectives.

1 Starter activities initiating whole-class discussion. Questioning will enable you to find out what the students already know.

2 Further details or extra 'fun facts' to support those listed in the *Student Book*.

3 More activities that can be used instead of or as well as those in the 'Things to do' section.

9 References to the corresponding *Student Book* pages and further information to expand on the paragraphs in the *Student Book*.

4 An activity or series of questions to help reinforce the main objectives in the plenary session to draw the lesson to a close.

8 Any additional information necessary for the activities in the 'Things to do' section of the *Student Book*, plus suggestions of how to differentiate and record.

5 Ideas for how students could present their work or tips for classroom displays.

7 Safety tips warning of possible hazards where appropriate.

6 The answer to the 'I wonder...' question, with additional background explanations if necessary.

The second type of lesson offers a challenge to encourage students to use their scientific enquiry skills to investigate a problem in context.

1 Starter activities initiate whole-class discussion.

2 List of materials that students will need, including any that need to be prepared in advance.

3 Information on how to organize, record, analyse and present data collected in the investigation. Spreadsheet tables for recording results and exemplar data to convert into charts can be found in the *Student Book* and *Workbook*.

4 More activities that can be used instead of or as well as the investigative challenge.

8 The challenge introduces the context and explains what students will be investigating.

7 Further details of how to carry out the investigation to support the instructions to the students in the *Student Book*.

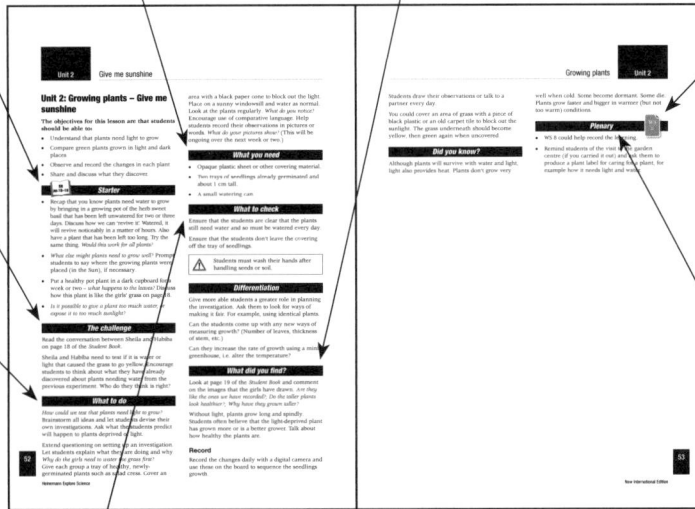

5 An activity or series of questions to help reinforce the main objectives in the plenary session to draw the lesson to a close.

6 Explanations of what students should be looking for and noticing, or how they should keep the test fair. Ideas on how to support and extend students are also included.

At the end of each Unit, material is provided for an assessment and review lesson.

2 Assessment sheets can be found in the *Workbook*.

1 A clear summary of the knowledge and skills students have gained throughout the Unit.

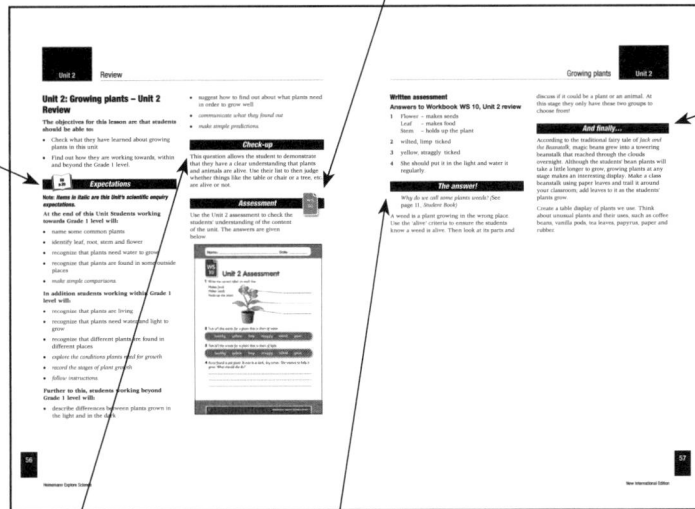

3 A final activity completes the Unit to remind students of everything they have learned.

5 Explanation and expected responses to the 'Check-up' in the *Student Book*.

4 The answer to the original question posed at the beginning of the Unit. Discuss what the students think now in light of what they have learned.

5

How to use
Heinemann Explore Science

For ease of use, *Heinemann Explore Science* follows the structure of the Cambridge Primary Science Curriculum Framework, 2011. *Heinemann Explore Science* has been written so that you can be flexible about what you teach and when.

Heinemann Explore Science is more manageable than many primary science schemes. It has a simple structure, but it also offers wide investigative and research opportunities. A range of engaging tasks is offered for each topic, including practical and research-based activities. Its clear progression and layout offers more support to less confident teachers. Integrated assessment gives indications of how to interpret levels of attainment. There is support for differentiation with suggestions for extra challenges for bright students and support for students struggling with science concepts. There is both experimental and investigative science through reliable practical investigations.

Heinemann Explore Science emphasizes: investigations; the clear use of strong vocabulary lists; building on students' ideas and addressing common misconceptions through questioning and discussion; clearly identified support and extend activities; class demonstration as a basis for some practical activities; and appropriate activities as part of students' homework. It offers flexibility of use; although Units are ordered to match the Cambridge Curriculum Framework, they can be taught in any order to suit a school's own scheme of work. This helps in mixed-age classes.

Differentiation

Within any class there will be a wide range of experience and ability. In a mixed-age class that range is further extended. This is a challenge to any teacher, and many address it through careful differentiation. Commonly, work is planned for a number of different groups (often three: high achievers, a middle range group, and students needing additional support). Teachers then allocate their resources – human and practical – to these groups to ensure the best possible outcome for everybody. This 'planning for differentiation' is demanding, and may leave feelings of dissatisfaction – 'I didn't spend long enough with the high-fliers/slower group today', 'I hope I'm not neglecting the majority of the class'. Some teachers have similar difficulties with 'differentiation by outcome'. Less able students may be unchallenged by the assumption that they will always produce a few lines of text when others routinely write a page.

Heinemann Explore Science expects that you will need to differentiate your work, and so a range of resources is offered, any of which may stimulate particular groups. You may choose to: present an activity on an investigation table, possibly supported by an informed adult; to set out resources that students can use for creative play; or to use the *Student Book* or *Workbook* for stimulus, for direction or for recording.

The 'starting off' activities in *Heinemann Explore Science* invite a third form of differentiation: differentiation by presentation. This is so familiar to teachers that few recognize how effectively they use it. The way in which a topic is presented engages students, but it also enables you to assess their prior knowledge. Because of its practical nature, students who may not shine in other subjects will often contribute more in science. Students who are able in every respect may still surprise you with their knowledge, but this 'knowledge' needs to be probed carefully – a superficial knowledge may lack the depth of understanding on which new science learning can be built.

That's why *Heinemann Explore Science* includes a number of exemplar questions to elicit current understanding – whether it is insecure, or even whether students have misconceptions that need gently challenging. It is when you group the students and set the tasks that you 'differentiate by presentation' – an unconscious and instinctive skill that results in different groups busily engaged with differing levels of support and monitoring.

Level statements to help you identify at which level students are working are provided in this *Teacher's Book*, for each Unit. These are also provided at the back of the *Student Book* for discussion and as checklists to enable self-assessment by students.

Heinemann Explore Science contains a wide range of ideas for interaction that includes things to do, questions to ask and resources to support learning. Your professional role is in the effective deployment of those resources.

The Heinemann Explore Science website

This provides a full range of editable planning materials, generic writing frames and presentation templates to support students in recording and presenting their work.

The website also provides digital e-book versions of all the *Readers* for each Grade and for the *Student Book* and *Workbooks*, so that worksheets can be downloaded and printed if needed.

Using ICT for research

Students should develop their research skills using a variety of secondary sources. Throughout the *Student Book*, students are given opportunities to use ICT (Information and Communication Technology) to research the answers to questions related to the topic of the lesson. At the end of each Unit, a more open question with reference only to the appropriate area of study is introduced to encourage students to develop search skills and strategies.

The Heinemann Explore Science Readers

These have been written bearing in mind the language needs of students for whom English is not a first language. Each book complements a Unit in the scheme. They offer interesting illustrations and simple, engaging text. Word count increases with higher grades. They can be used as individual Readers, books to read at home, or for group reading. They can be used for vocabulary and language exercise, and there are suggestions for activities at the back of each book – from crosswords to team games.

Living Things, a Grade 1 science Reader, features plants and animals that should be familiar to students living in Southern Asia and the Middle East.

Used alongside the other components of the scheme, they offer opportunities for developing science and language, hand-in-hand.

Health and safety Issues

Primary science is a very safe activity, but that does not mean that you should not consider health and safety issues when you plan, or that you should feel unsupported, either. ***Heinemann Explore Science*** highlights specific safety issues in lessons when appropriate, and you should also engage in your own risk assessment and take appropriate precautions. This should not be demanding; it involves looking at your students, your circumstances and support staff, and ensuring that you have noted, minimized and if necessary recorded any apparent hazards. It is essential to share this risk assessment with other adults in the classroom.

Every adult on the school site should be familiar with the school's Health and Safety Policy, and especially how it reflects on their responsibilities. They should know the location and proper use of safety equipment. All adults have a responsibility for their own safety, and that of their students in school, whatever their age. This is a responsibility you share with others. Teaching assistants, for example, are often responsible for small groups of students doing practical activities – their supervision may be vital where a hazard has been recognized, for example, when using a cooker. Working with a small group like this offers opportunities not just for realistic but negative teaching ('Don't touch that – it's hot!') but also for positive modelling of safe behaviour ('Now how should I pick this up?')

You can give a very positive image of health and safety issues by performing a routine risk assessment while planning an activity, and encouraging students to make their own assessment of risk, and take their own precautions. Engaging students in safety planning helps them to understand the importance of not taking risks. If students are simply told what is safe without explanation they are less likely to take it as seriously as when they are themselves involved in safety planning.

Here are a few general commonsense reminders:

Food: Eating and drinking is forbidden in school science labs, but some of primary science is concerned with food – science activities may require students to eat, but only with your permission. Fingers do get sucked, and foods are tempting. Ensure that guidelines on 'what to eat' are clear and take into account both ethnicity, custom, parental wishes and allergies.

New International Edition

Present the best practice in food handling: the cleaning and/or covering of tables, and the use of cooking utensils kept only for this purpose. Pupils should know not to enter the food area unless they are in the practical group (mark or point out an area that can only be entered with clean hands and wearing an apron). Protective clothing not only keeps the students' clothes clean but also prevents food contamination. It should be kept solely for food use.

Laminated plastic tables are ideal. Wooden tables (or damaged laminated tables) should be covered with clean plastic tablecloths kept specifically for food. Older students can use antibacterial cleaners after an initial thorough clean by an adult. Spray or wipe all food preparation surfaces including chopping boards with the antibacterial cleaner.

Nobody – pupil or adult – should work with food if they are unwell, including sickness, diarrhoea, colds, coughs and other infections. Cuts must be covered with a clean waterproof dressing – blue plasters show up if they drop into food! Supervise students washing hands before food work, or after using the toilet. Provide colourless, perfume-free liquid soap and running water. If a hot air dryer is not available, provide disposable paper towels or paper roller towels. Discourage students from touching their face, hair or other parts of their body, and from coughing or sneezing over food.

Electricity: Teach students about the dangers of mains electricity. Students live with electricity and refusing them experience of it is comparable to not teaching them road safety rules for fear of traffic accidents. Mains electricity has a far greater 'push' round the circuit than battery electricity. It is this greater push that kills. The human body is not a good conductor of electricity, but it conducts electricity far better when wet. Work with low-voltage 'battery' electricity is not risky.

Forces: Many activities in science (and technology) put students at risk because little thought is given to possible outcomes. What will happen if the elastic band snaps, the bag breaks, or the liquid spills? Students may take unnecessary risks too, by not using basic science equipment (eye protection, a cutting board or bench hook) that could keep them safe. Testing-to-breaking-point activities in topics such as Forces can be

dangerous unless students have considered the consequences of breakage.

Animals: The key factor is the welfare of both students and animals. The learning outcome is an understanding of animal welfare and a positive educational experience of (say) a small mammal. It's important to ensure that none of the students has an allergy to animal fur. If you introduce family pets, it's unlikely that they are used to being surrounded by a group of excited students.

Introduce any animal to a group/class yourself. Talk about them, drawing out what the students know, and what they think about how the animal might behave. Students empathize with small animals, and will understand that they could be easily frightened.

The adult should handle the animal throughout the group activity. Students could ask their questions first, and then take it in turns to stroke the animal at the end, which reduces the chances that students will go rubbing their eyes or sucking their fingers afterwards! After their experience, they should wash their hands again, under supervision.

General advice: Younger students can be expected to be able to control risks to themselves and others. They commonly know what is dangerous. Classroom accidents are frequently the result of students forgetting what is sensible because they are caught up in an activity, especially if it is exciting science!

Essential safety advice is contained in a book from the Association for Science Education called *'Be Safe!'* and every teacher should be aware of it and its contents. *Be Safe!* is available from:
The Association for Science Education, College Lane, Hatfield, Herts. AL10 9AA, UK

www.ase.org.uk
Be Safe! ISBN: 978 0 86357 426 9

CLEAPSS is the advisory service for health and safety in science education. CLEAPSS offers informative publications, a staffed helpline, and a members' website. It is an essential source of science safety knowledge.

www.cleapss.org.uk

Curriculum structure of *Heinemann Explore Science*

Heinemann Explore Science has been very carefully structured to ensure a progressive development in the students using the course, both of scientific process skills and also of knowledge and understanding. This complements the approach taken in the Cambridge Primary Science Curriculum Framework (2011).

The development of scientific process skills throughout the complete course is shown in this skills ladder:

Heinemann Explore Science Science Skills Ladder

Skills Domain	Year 1 Children have opportunities:	Year 2 Children have opportunities:	Year 3 Children have opportunities:	Year 4 Children have opportunities:	Year 5 Children have opportunities:	Year 6 Children have opportunities:
1. **Ideas and evidence in science**	to collect evidence to try and answer a question	to collect evidence to try and answer a question	to collect evidence in a variety of contexts to answer a question or test an idea	to collect evidence in a variety of contexts to test an idea or prediction based on their scientific knowledge and understanding	to consider how scientists have combined evidence from observation and measurement with creative thinking to suggest new ideas and explanations for phenomena	to consider how scientists have combined evidence from observation and measurement with creative thinking to suggest new ideas and explanations for phenomena
2. **Investigative skills** **Planning investigative work**	to test ideas suggested to them and say what they think will happen	to suggest some ideas and questions based on simple knowledge and say how they might find out about them; to say what they think might happen; and to think about and discuss whether comparisons and tests are fair or unfair	in a variety of contexts, to suggest questions and ideas and how to test them; to make predictions about what will happen; to think about how to collect sufficient evidence in some contexts; and to consider what makes a test unfair or evidence sufficient and, with help, plan fair tests	to suggest questions that can be tested and make predictions about what will happen, some of which are based on scientific knowledge; to design a fair test or plan how to collect sufficient evidence; and, in some contexts, to choose what apparatus to use and what to measure	to make predictions of what will happen based on scientific knowledge and understanding, and suggest how to test these; to use knowledge and understanding to plan how to carry out a fair test or how to collect sufficient evidence to test an idea; and to identify factors that need to be taken into consideration in different contexts	to decide how to turn ideas into a form that can be tested and, where appropriate, to make predictions using scientific knowledge and understanding; to identify factors that are relevant to a particular situation; to choose what evidence to collect to investigate a question, ensuring the evidence is sufficient; and to choose what equipment to use

9

Heinemann Explore Science Science Skills Ladder

Skills Domain	Year 1 Children have opportunities:	Year 2 Children have opportunities:	Year 3 Children have opportunities:	Year 4 Children have opportunities:	Year 5 Children have opportunities:	Year 6 Children have opportunities:
3. **Obtaining and presenting evidence**		to make observations using appropriate senses; to make some measurements of length using standard and non-standard measures; and to present some findings in simple tables and block graphs	to make observations and comparisons; to measure length, volume of liquid and time in standard measures using simple measuring equipment effectively; and to present results in drawing, bar charts and tables	to make observations and comparisons of relevant features in a variety of contexts; to make measurements of temperature, time and force as well as measurements of length; to begin to think about why measurements of length should be repeated; and to present results in bar charts and tables	to make relevant observations; to consolidate measurement of volume, temperature, time and length; to measure pulse rate; to think about why observations and measurements should be repeated; and to present results in bar charts and line graphs	to make a variety of relevant observations and measurements using simple apparatus correctly; to decide when observations and measurements need to be checked, by repeating, to give more reliable data; and to use tables, bar charts and line graphs to present results
4. **Considering evidence and approach**	to communicate observations orally, in drawing, by labelling and in simple writing; to make simple comparisons and groupings that relate to differences and similarities between living things and objects; in some cases to say what their observations show, and whether it was what they expected; and to draw simple conclusions and explain what they did	to make simple comparisons, identifying similarities and differences between living things, objects and events; to say what results show; to say whether their predictions were supported; in some cases to use knowledge to explain what was found out and to draw conclusions; and to explain what they did	to draw conclusions from results and begin to use scientific knowledge to suggest explanations for them; and to make generalisations and begin to identify simple patterns in results presented in tables	to identify simple trends and patterns in results presented in tables, charts and graphs and to suggest explanations for some of these; to explain what the evidence shows and whether it supports any predictions made; and to link the evidence to scientific knowledge and understanding in some contexts	to decide whether results support any prediction; to begin to evaluate repeated results; to recognise and make predictions from patterns in data and suggest explanations for these using scientific knowledge and understanding; to interpret data and think about whether it is sufficient to draw conclusions; and to draw conclusions indicating whether these match any prediction made	to make comparisons; to evaluate repeated results; to identify patterns in results and results that do not appear to fit the pattern; to use results to draw conclusions and to make further predictions; to suggest and evaluate explanations for these predictions using scientific knowledge and understanding; and to say whether the evidence supports any prediction made

Heinemann Explore Science Curriculum Matching Chart for Grade 1

This chart show where all of the topics and Learning Outcomes specified in the Cambridge Primary Science Curriculum Framework (2011) are covered in the *Heinemann Explore Science* course.

Learning Objectives	*Student Book* coverage	Supporting coverage in *Teacher's Book* or *Workbook*
Scientific enquiry		
Scientific enquiry: Ideas and evidence		
Try to answer questions by collecting evidence through observation.	Unit 3 Sorting and using materials • Common materials pp.24–5	*Teacher's Book* 1, pp.58–79
	Unit 4 Forces • Using pushes and pulls pp.36–7	*Teacher's Book* 1, pp.80–101
	Unit 5 Sound • Where is quietest? pp.47–8	*Teacher's Book* 1, pp.102–121
Scientific enquiry: Plan investigative work		
Ask questions and contribute to discussions about how to seek answers.	Unit 2 Growing plants • Thirsty plants p.16 • Give me sunshine pp.17–18 • Seeds inside p.19	*Teacher's Book* 1, pp.38–57
	Unit 4 Forces • Using pushes and pulls pp.36–7	*Teacher's Book* 1, pp.80–101
Make predictions.	Unit 5 Sound • Where is quietest? pp.47–8 • Is bigger better? pp.51–52	*Teacher's Book* 1, pp.102–121
Decide what to do to try to answer a science question.	Unit 2 Growing plants • Plant parts p.14 • Leaves and roots p.15 • Thirsty plants p.16	*Teacher's Book* 1, pp.38–57
	Unit 3 Sorting and using materials • Common materials pp.24–25 • All bagged up pp.30–1	*Teacher's Book* 1, pp.58–79
	Unit 5 Sound • All ears p.5 • Is bigger better? pp.51–3	*Teacher's Book* 1, pp.102–121
Scientific enquiry: Obtain and present evidence		
Explore and observe in order to collect evidence (measurements and observations) to answer questions.	Unit 1 Ourselves and other animals • Give me five senses p.6 • I'm sensitive p.7 • Growing older p.8	*Teacher's Book* 1, pp.16–37
	Unit 2 Growing plants • Plenty of plants p.13 • Plant parts p.14 • Leaves and roots p.15 • Seeds inside p.19	*Teacher's Book* 1, pp.38–57
	Unit 3 Sorting and using materials • What's it like? p.22 • A lot of materials p.23	*Teacher's Book* 1, pp.58–79

	Unit 4 Forces • Using pushes and pulls pp.36–7 • How far can you go? pp.38–39	*Teacher's Book* 1, pp.80–102
	Unit 5 Sound • Diminishing distances p.54–5	*Teacher's Book* 1, pp.102–121
Suggest ideas and follow instructions.	**Unit 1 Ourselves and other animals** • I'm special! p.2 • Healthy food p.4 • Staying healthy p.5 • Give me five senses p.6 • I'm sensitive p.7 • Growing older p.8 • We all grow p.9	*Teacher's Book* 1, pp.16–37
	Unit 2 Growing plants • Dead or alive? p.12 • Plenty of plants p.13 • Plant parts p.14 • Leaves and roots p.15 • Seeds inside p.19	*Teacher's Book* 1, pp.38–57
	Unit 3 Sorting and using materials • What's it like? p.22 • A lot of materials p.23 • Common materials pp.24–5 • The properties of materials p.26 • What's its job? p.27 • Don't get wet p.28 • Paper p.29	*Teacher's Book* 1, pp.38–57
	Unit 4 Forces • Moving around p.34 • Moving things around p.35 • Slow down p.40 • Other ways of moving things p.41 • Which way next? p.42 • Blow football p.43	*Teacher's Book* 1, pp.80–101
	Unit 5 Sound • Sounds all around p.46 • Where is quietest? pp.47–48 • All ears p.50 • Is bigger better? pp.51–2 • Sounds far away p.53 • Diminishing distances pp.54–5	*Teacher's Book* 1, pp.102–121
Scientific enquiry: Consider evidence and approach		
Make comparisons.	**Unit 1 Ourselves and other animals** • I'm special! p.2 • Who's tallest? p.3 • Growing older p.8 • We all grow p.9	*Teacher's Book* 1, pp.18–39
	Unit 2 Growing plants • Dead or alive? p.12 • Plant parts p.14 • Leaves and roots p.15	*Teacher's Book* 1, pp.40–59 *Teacher's Book* 1, pp.60–81
	Unit 3 Sorting and using materials • Paper p.29	

Compare what happened with predictions.	Unit 5 Sound • Where is quietest? pp.47–8 • Is bigger better? pp.51–2	*Teacher's Book* 1, pp.104–123
Model and communicate ideas in order to share, explain and develop them.	Unit 1 Ourselves and other animals • Who's tallest? p.3	*Teacher's Book* 1, pp.16–37
	Unit 2 Growing plants • Thirsty plants p.16 • Give me sunshine pp.17–8	*Teacher's Book* 1, pp.38–57
	Unit 3 Sorting and using materials • All bagged up pp.30–1	*Teacher's Book* 1, pp.58–79
	Unit 4 Forces • Using pushes and pulls pp.36–7 • How far can you go? pp.38–9	*Teacher's Book* 1, pp.80–101
	Unit 5 Sound • Where is quietest? pp.47–8 • Is bigger better? pp.51–2 • Diminishing distances pp.54–5	*Teacher's Book* 1, pp.102–121

Biology

Biology: Plants

Know that plants are living things.	Unit 2 Growing plants • Dead or alive? p.12 • Plenty of plants p.13	*Teacher's Book* 1, pp.38–57
Know that there are living things and things that have never been alive.	Unit 1 Ourselves and other animals • I'm special! p.2	*Teacher's Book* 1, pp.16–37
	Unit 2 Growing plants • Dead or alive? p.12	*Teacher's Book* 1, pp.38–57 *Workbook* 1, p.1
Explore ways that different animals and plants inhabit local environments.	Unit 2 Growing plants • Plenty of plants p.13 • Plant parts p.14	*Teacher's Book* 1, pp.16–37
Name the major parts of a plant, looking at real plants and models.	Unit 2 Growing plants • Plant parts p.14	*Teacher's Book* 1, pp.38–57
Know that plants need light and water to grow.	Unit 2 Growing plants • Dead or alive? p.12 • Leaves and roots p.15 • Thirsty plants p.16 • Give me sunshine pp.17–8	*Teacher's Book* 1, pp.38–57 *Workbook* 1, p.7
Explore how seeds grow into flowering plants.	Unit 2 Growing plants • Seeds inside p.19	*Teacher's Book* 1, pp.38–57 *Workbook* 1, pp.8–9

Biology: Humans and animals

Recognize the similarities and differences between each other.	Unit 1 Ourselves and other animals • I'm special! p.2 • Who's tallest? p.3	*Teacher's Book* 1, pp.16–37
Recognize and name the main external parts of the body.	Unit 1 Ourselves and other animals • I'm special! p.2	*Teacher's Book* 1, pp.16–37
Know about the need for a healthy diet, including the right types of food and water.	Unit 1 Ourselves and other animals • Healthy food p.4 • Staying healthy p.5	*Teacher's Book* 1, pp.16–37 *Workbook* 1, p.2

13

Explore how senses enable humans and animals to be aware of the world around them.	Unit 1 Ourselves and other animals • Give me five senses p.6 • I'm sensitive p.7	*Teacher's Book* 1, pp.16–37 *Workbook* 1, p.3
Know that humans and animals produce offspring which grow into adults.	Unit 1 Ourselves and other animals • Growing older p.8 • We all grow p.9	*Teacher's Book* 1, pp.16–37 *Workbook* 1, p.4–5
Chemistry		
Chemistry: Material properties		
Use senses to explore and talk about different materials.	Unit 3 Sorting and using materials • What's it like? p.22	*Teacher's Book* 1, pp.58–79
Identify the characteristics of different materials.	Unit 3 Sorting and using materials • A lot of materials p.23 • Common materials pp.24–5 • The properties of materials p.26	*Teacher's Book* 1, pp.58–79 *Workbook* 1, pp.12–13
Recognize and name common materials.	Unit 3 Sorting and using materials • What's it like? p.22 • A lot of materials p.23 • Common materials pp.24–5 • The properties of materials p.26 • What's its job? p.27 • Don't get wet p.28 • Paper p.29 • All bagged up pp.30–1	*Teacher's Book* 1, pp.58–79 *Workbook* 1, pp.11–13
Sort objects into groups based on the properties of their materials.	Unit 3 Sorting and using materials • A lot of materials p.23 • Common materials pp.24–5 • Don't get wet p.28 • Paper p.29	*Teacher's Book* 1, pp.58–79
Physics		
Physics: Forces		
Explore, talk about and describe the movement of familiar things.	Unit 4 Forces • Moving around p.34 • Moving things around p.35	*Teacher's Book* 1, pp.80–101
Recognize that both pushes and pulls are forces.	Unit 4 Forces • Using pushes and pulls pp.36–7 • How far can you go? pp.38–9	*Teacher's Book* 1, pp.80–101 *Workbook* 1, p.15
Recognize that when things speed up, slow down or change direction there is a cause.	Unit 4 Forces • Slow down p.40 • Other ways of moving things p.41 • Which way next? p.42 • Blow football p.43	*Teacher's Book* 1, pp.80–101 *Workbook* 1, pp.16–17
Physics: Sound		
Identify many sources of sound.	Unit 5 Sound • Sounds all around p.46 • Where is quietest? pp.47–8 • Music makers p.49	*Teacher's Book* 1, pp.102–121 *Workbook* 1, p.19
Know that we hear when sound enters our ear.	Unit 5 Sound • All ears p.50 • Is bigger better? pp.51–2	*Teacher's Book* 1, pp.102–121
Recognize that as sound travels from a source it becomes fainter.	Unit 5 Sound • Diminishing distances pp.54–5	*Teacher's Book* 1, pp.102–121 *Workbook* 1, p.20

Resources for *Heinemann Explore Science* Grade 1

The following list gives details of resources needed for activities suggested in the lessons (over and above those normally available in the classroom). You will only need some of them, depending on the activities you choose to use and how many students will be doing them.

Science equipment and durable items

alarm clocks
bells
butterfly cage
digital camera
droppers
garden hose pipe
gardening tools
magnets
music tapes/CDs including
 Benjamin Britten's *Young
 Person's Guide to the Orchestra*
 and Prokofiev's *Peter and the
 Wolf*

plaster of Paris
plastic fabrics
plastic sheet
pouches
range of different musical
 instruments – tuned and
 untuned percussion, wind and
 string, as well as ones from
 different cultures
recordings of different sounds,
 including animal noises
rope
sound meter

tank for frogspawn
tape recorder or CD player
tapes or CDs of common sounds
tricycle or cart
trundle wheel
vacuum cleaner hose
wax
weights
whistles
wooden blocks
woven fabrics

Consumables and items locally available

adult and baby clothes
aluminium cans
artificial flower/plant
baby bottles
baby clothes
battery-operated toys
blindfolds
books or videos involving
 builders, e.g. Bob the Builder
cards with a range of facial
features
clip board
clockwork toys
cups or kitchen jugs
drinking straws
earmuffs
face shape templates
fertilised chicken eggs
floor turtle, e.g. Roamer
fruit seeds, like pumpkin or
 melon
geraniums

greaseproof paper
images of things that make
 sounds around the school
jam jars or other food jars
musical instruments
nappies
newspaper weather maps
packets of seeds – flowers and
 vegetables
paper ranging from A5 to A2
paper towels
pebbles in a bottle
petroleum jelly
photographs of all stages in the
 human life cycle
plant bulbs, e.g. hyacinth, onion
plastic bags
potted plants – various types and
 sizes, including a pot-bound
 plant, a tomato plant and cacti
 leaves, and a large cabbage
 (red or green)

salad cress seedlings germinated
sand
seed catalogues
seeds and seed casings, e.g.
 coconuts, poppies, pine-
 cones, bird seed, vegetables
 (cauliflower, broccoli, celery,
 spinach)
selection of bean seeds, e.g. broad
 beans, mung beans
sheets of wallpaper or lining
 paper
small spoons (baby)
steel cans
sweet basil
toy bricks
toy cars
vegetable oil
writing paper

15

Unit 1: Ourselves and other animals

The objectives for this Unit are that students should be able to:

- Recognise the similarities and differences between each other

- Know about the need for a healthy diet, including the right types of food, and water

- Identify and locate different parts of their body

- Be able to name their senses and how we are aware of the world around us

- Understand that humans and animals grow in similar ways producing offspring which grow into adults

- Communicate what they can see, what they are doing and what they found out.

SB pp.1–10 **Science background**

This may be the first science Unit students meet as part of their science education. Remember that most of their past experience will be relevant; answering 'why?' questions with a practical activity is the essence of science at any stage.

Being alive

We take it for granted that we are alive. As humans we demonstrate seven essential life processes:

1. we take in and use food for energy

2. we move

3. we grow but we don't expand like a balloon; we add material to our bodies

4. we can reproduce

5. we respire – breathing is the movement of air; the whole process is called respiration

6. we respond to stimuli, using our senses to gain awareness of what is going on around us and responding accordingly

7. we produce waste.

Our bodies are all built on a similar pattern, but with apparently endless variety. Students need to know the names, and later the functions, at first of the external parts of the body, and later of the parts that are hidden from view.

Five senses

By 'senses' we mean the ways in which we experience things around us. There are five familiar senses: sight, hearing, smell, taste and touch. These senses are all receivers. We do not see or hear actively. We collect light in our eyes and sound in our ears. This is a mature concept and goes against everything we commonly say; for example: 'I can see through this window'. Understanding that our eyes receive available light, and our ears environmental sound, will underpin later work on sound and light. Some senses commonly work together – taste and smell, for example – and this can complicate understanding.

There is evidence that young children use different models for seeing objects compared with seeing light from a lamp. For example they use a 'light to the eye' model for light sources. Yet they often use an 'active seeing/magic beams' model for seeing other objects. Some children think – perhaps because they have been told that a dimly-lit room is 'dark' – that they can see in the dark.

We hear sounds when vibrations in the air reach our ear. Our ear is sensitive to vibrations, and the brain converts them to the sensations we know. It's a common misconception that covering your ears actually makes your voice quieter – that's just the effect it has on you.

All smells are made from seven basic smells in different combinations of intensity. The seven smells are:

- ethereal

- floral

- mothball

- musk

- peppermint

- pungent

- putrid.

We recognize these because we have seven different types of sensor. Your sense of smell makes your sense of taste a great deal more accurate. Smells from your food reach your nose while you are eating. When you have a cold, your nose is blocked and your food tastes dull. This is because the sticky mucus we all produce masks the smell cells.

Skin is the organ of touch. Our bodies are covered in millions of nerve endings that are sensitive to different forms of stimuli – touch, heat, cold, pressure and pain. There are greater or lesser numbers of nerve endings, depending on where they are on the body, so our lips and fingertips have far more detectors than the small of our back.

Remind students that we are able to feel with all parts of our body, not just with our hands.

Humans as animals

Humans are animals, with all the characteristics of other animals. Like all animals, humans grow. Children may believe that their bodies expand like balloons, or that they grow only on their birthdays, or when they are measured. Emphasize that growth is the constant process of adding to your body, and the growth process takes years. For this reason, human young need care and guidance that far exceeds the demands of some other animals. Frogs and other amphibians and insects, for example, are independent from birth, while birds and small mammals depend on parental support for a short time. Compare this with the 16 years or more that we usually devote to our children!

It is usually easy to match adults and their young, but for some animals, like frogs, caddis flies, dragonflies and butterflies, the different stages in their life history perform different life functions such as eating and growing, or reproducing. This process is called metamorphosis. We all grow at different rates and with different results. For instance, around the age of five girls are often taller than boys, but this is not true of every boy and girl. Ensure the students understand that although there are 'average rates and ranges', there are no absolutes concerning human growth.

Living and not living

We distinguish living things from those that are not alive by their ability to carry out many of the life processes mentioned earlier. Children often find it difficult to distinguish living things from other things that move, or grow by expanding. They tend to overemphasize movement as a criterion for life and so may believe that flames and clouds are alive. At this stage, a child's process of understanding will take some time to mature. Challenge students with questions like: 'When did this apple die?' or, 'Is a cloud a plant or an animal?' to provoke their thinking.

There are differences between us all – even identical twins. Impress upon students that these differences are what make us all special and they are to be celebrated, rather than derided. You could use hair colour variation as an example. Information like this can be recorded in different visual ways and students can see this illustrated in simple brick towers and bar charts.

Life needs sustaining and students will learn that, without the right conditions, care and sustenance, plants and animals die. Understanding in this area leads to later work on balanced diet, exercise and general body care.

Language

Alive Able to grow, have young and change when their environment changes.

Bar chart A graph, where the length of each bar stands for a separate piece of data.

Bitter A harsh taste, like coffee.

Ear The sense organ that receives sound.

Eye The sense organ that receives light.

Grow To get bigger by adding to yourself.

Human One special kind of animal.

Pictogram A graph, where each picture represents a separate piece of data.

Offspring The young of an animal or plant.

Salty Tasting of salt.

Sense One of the five ways we find out about the world.

Sour A sharp taste, like lemon.

Sweet Tasting of sugar or honey.

Key vocabulary

The following words might be introduced or used with the children alongside others, to accustom them to the nature of scientific vocabulary:

communicate	measure
compare	observe
describe	predict
explain	record
like	show

New International Edition

These words may be of use in terms of comparisons:

animal	old/older/oldest
arm	ourselves
beak	sight
different	similar
feel	smell
hear	tall/taller/tallest
human	taste
leg	touch
living	wing
myself	young/younger/youngest

Resources

A full list of resources is located at the end of the introduction to the *Teacher's Book* for ease of gathering resources (page 15). Many will already be in the classroom, but a few may need prior arrangement. For example,

- Child-sized sheets of wallpaper or lining paper for students to draw their own body outlines.

- Prepared face shape templates with basic features already present.

- A set of cards with a range of facial features in different colours and shapes for students to choose from.

- A tank for frogspawn to hatch out in or a butterfly cage to keep caterpillars and butterflies in, or even small fish or giant land snails.

- Some fertilized chicken eggs. To hatch out some chicks – keeping a running record of their development with drawings and photographs. This will help with the last lesson in the Unit. There are no reasons for not keeping other animals in the classroom. For example, stick insects, ants or fish. These could be used as part of the life cycles of other animals.

- Cassette tapes or CDs of common sounds.

- A selection of adult and baby clothes (the students could bring some in).

- Photographs of all stages in the human life cycle, from a baby to a very old person (you could ask the students to bring in pictures of this or use staff members, which always raises a giggle!).

- The readers *Ourselves* and *Living Things* may be used with this Unit. Note that some of the animals shown in *Living Things* go beyond the Cambridge curriculum for Grade 1. Ask children if they have seen animals like these, or know their names, but do not trouble the students with learning the names.

Bright ideas

- Playing 'Simon Says' is a favourite game and could be used throughout science to reinforce different parts of the body, becoming more complex with the parts asked to be named. You could also sing the song 'Head, Shoulders Knees and Toes', adding other body parts in and seeing how fast you can go.

- Another game that could be played is 'Guess Who', where the students have to use observable features to eliminate other faces to 'guess who' the face is that's picked. Happy families may also be a fun game to play to spot the similarities, but also to develop questioning, in terms of the 'right' type of question.

- Other investigations that you might like to try are:

  Is the person with the biggest shoe size the tallest?

  Measure around your head. How many times does that measurement fit into the measurement of your height?

  Do our body shapes change as we get older? (The proportion of head size to body length changes.)

  About half of us can roll our tongue lengthways when we stick it out – can you?

Knowledge check

Most children this age should be able to name their main body parts in their first language.

You cannot assume their knowledge of colours or the vocabulary to explain what they see, hear, touch, taste and smell.

Skills check

Students need to:

- be encouraged to explain to you what they observe.

- explain what they are doing.

- tell you what they expect.

- tell you what they found out.

- be encouraged to make comparisons: taller than, bigger than, louder than, softer than.

- distinguish different uses – tall and big, heavy and large.

- be able to define words clearly; especially if they have more than one meaning, for example light, smell, like.

As a teacher, always try to ask 'open' questions: 'What did you hear?' rather than 'Did you hear that?'.

Links to other subjects

Young children are very egotistical, and you might argue that everything they study at this age is an aspect of 'Ourselves'. Possible links include:

Literacy: Read and use captions and labels. Write captions and labels for their own work. Follow simple instructions. Make simple lists and write simple instructions. Tell their brief autobiography, changes and developments in their lives. Talk about a new baby – additions to the family.

Numeracy: Opportunities for counting up to, and beyond, ten. Read, write and order numbers. Comparisons of length, weight and volume. Suggest and use suitable non-standard and standard units. Ordering by size.

Physical education: PE is the obvious connection, giving students opportunities to use their bodies and senses. Name body parts. Ask for different movements. Name the joints – neck, elbow, hip, knee, ankle – that enable body movement, and explore the degree of movement possible.

Food technology: Cookery can be linked to work on the senses: smells and tastes, for example.

Let's find out...

The Unit opens with this question:

Can you tell who someone is, without looking?

This question will be revisited at the end and will help to establish that we can use other senses if we can't use the 'usual' one.

Unit 1: Ourselves and other animals – I'm special!

The objectives for this lesson are that students should be able to:

- Recognize that their bodies have the same parts, and that there is a wide variety of body shapes and sizes

- Recognize and name external parts of the body

- Communicate their findings in simple ways

- Observe and draw their faces and compare the results.

SB p.2 — Starter

- Talk about our bodies and how we are all special. Ask students to name some of the (external) parts of the body.

- Make a list of vocabulary on a large sheet of paper. Keep for future use, using a different colour to indicate new words.

- Refer to the students' list of body parts. Use a student to name and match main parts of the body. *What are the children doing? Which parts of their bodies are they using?* The body parts list should include things such as: head, shoulders, knees, toes, elbow, hands, arm, leg, foot, fingers, neck, eyes, ears, nose, mouth.

Explain

Alive or not

Students may not be able to distinguish living and non-living things successfully. At this stage they only need to clarify that living things eat, grow and move. This creates a problem with plants as they can only be seen to grow slowly. A car could be classified as 'alive' as it moves! It is better to indicate that plants 'move' with the wind (although this will be clarified in more detail in later grades) and make their own food. Water and nutrients are taken through the roots from the soil.

Are we the same?

By looking at the similarities and differences of humans we are trying to show that we all have the same basic features, but it is the smaller details that are different and allow us to be identified.

Things to do

- Use a mirror for the students to look closely at their faces. They will need a template with their face (oval) and eyes, ears, nose and mouth marked on. They then need to add their features: for example, eye colour, mouth colour, hair, freckles, moles and any other distinguishing marks.

- This could be made more sophisticated by providing different shaped ovals and shaped eyes to then choose the best shape for their partner's face.

- Provide a limited set of face shape cards, eye shape and colour cards, mouth shapes, hair lengths and colours and ask students to make up their own face first of all. They can then make up someone else they know and ask others to guess who it is.

Differentiation — WS 1

Less able students could complete WS 1 to assess if they recognize something as living or not.

Did you know?

All hair is a shade of brown and even red hair starts this way. It is the amount of pigment that decides the colour.

Dig deeper

This leads into the next lesson when the students look at the parts of the face and then the names of other body parts. They could complete a class survey or just find out the names of the colours: for example green, blue and brown.

I wonder...

Parents can recognize very small differences in identical twins. As the twins grow older these differences may become more apparent.

Other ideas

- Use stories and songs about bodies to introduce fictional variety in body shape and size. *What is this called? How many have you got?* (touching part or picture) *Which is longer? Bigger? Smaller? What do you use this for?* (touching part or picture).

- Draw around and label feet and shoes. Match feet and shoe cut-outs.

- Play 'Guess Who', the game where the students have to ask questions about what features might be present on the key chosen figure to eliminate the other characters on the board.

- Use the reader *Ourselves* with the class for further discussion on ways in which we are all the same and ways in which we are different.

Presentation

At the start of the year, use pictures or photographs of class members to create a getting-to-know-you, 'We're special!' class display.

Plenary

WS 1

- Use some famous or fictional faces on the board and only show a single feature. Ask students to 'Guess who?' *Which features allow you to guess more easily?*

- Provide images of pets the students may have and ask them which features of their face they may have the same, for example eyes, nose, ears, etc. And which or how they are different, for example the shapes, the colours, etc.

- If not already used, then WS 1 can help assess if something is alive or not.

- *Do teachers really have eyes in the backs of their heads? What would you use another arm/leg/eye/ear for?*

21

Unit 1: Ourselves and other animals – Who's tallest?

The objectives for this lesson are that students should be able to:

- Compare the heights of different children
- Make a prediction on who the oldest person is based on height
- Understand that the oldest person may not be the tallest person
- Record their results.

SB p.3 **Starter**

- Provide a series of pictures of children of different heights and ask them to match the ages to the height.
- The natural thing will be for the students to believe that the older you are the taller you will be. Have another image that you can add that may challenge this concept.
- Discuss who the oldest is in our class. Then produce a list of students' birthdays and months in order, so this can be used later. Use this to predict who they think could be tallest in their class.

The challenge

- Read the conversation on page 3 (top right) of the *Student Book* or ask students to read a speech bubble each, to practise their reading, speaking and listening skills. Ask students for their ideas about who might be right.
- Discuss how you could find out just using the students in the class. *What information do we need? How will we get it? What is the best way to do this?*
- Discuss also how we could share what was found out with another class.

What to do

Class 1 have considered only one method of finding out. They could just compare the oldest person's height with everyone else in the class as a direct comparison.

What you need

- A blank wall.
- Large pieces of paper.
- Or a large hall where the students can lie down instead of standing up.

What to check

The simplest method is for the students to line up in order of age. This may be challenging, but could be helped by first producing a list of students' birthdays. The students could line up in order of height and then ask the oldest to put their hand up. Either way is valid.

> ⚠ No known safety issues. Some sensitivity needs to be shown towards the size of students, to remove any stress or tension they might feel at this activity.

Differentiation

- More able students can measure the heights of the people being observed. This could be done in non-standard measures, for example string which is then laid out on the desk, or in hand-spans, stick lengths, or foot lengths, toe-to-toe, if the students are laid out on the floor. These students may also be able to organize the rest of the group into the continuum line without any help – the natural leaders of the group.
- Students who struggle with measuring will only need to make a comparison to say who is tallest and who shortest. Adult support for this activity may be required for this group, in terms of relating age to height.

What did you find?

The children of Class 1 discovered that the oldest person isn't always the tallest, but very nearly.

Is this the same with your class?

Record

- Photographs can be taken of the students lined up, and then used for comparison later.

- The wall could be marked (if it is covered in paper first!) to produce the 'chart'.

- Each child could use the cut-out of the previous activity of their bodies and then stick these on the wall in order of age, or order of height.

  Work from the face drawing to the body drawing to the height activity, building on each.

Did you know?

Humans continue to grow until their late teens or twenties. If you don't count putting on weight, then only our hair and nails can be seen to grow.

Plenary

- Your ears and nose continue to grow as you get older. Discuss with the students how they could record this! Or discuss how they could find out at what age people stop growing taller.

- There are lots of giants in children's books. There are also giant plants, like the redwood General Sherman in the Giant Forest of Sequoia National Park in Tulare County, California.

- *What if you never stopped growing? What would the problems be?*

New International Edition

Unit 1: Ourselves and other animals – Healthy food

The objectives for this lesson are that students should be able to:

- Recognize healthy and unhealthy foods
- Understand that our 'diet' is the food we eat
- Find out how to put food into groups
- Discuss healthy diets.

SB p.4 Starter

- Have an array of foods on the table, including chocolate, crisps, fruit, vegetables, takeaway boxes, rice, flat breads and so on – in fact anything you may have eaten last week! State that this is what you ate last week. Which food would the students like to eat themselves? Which food do they think they wouldn't like?

- Play the song 'Food glorious food' from *Oliver!* (the musical) and discuss the foods they are singing about.

Explain

Good food

Discuss what the foodstuffs are on the plate on page 4. Can the students recognize them? Do they think this is a good plate of food?

Discuss what they would swap any of the foods for. For example, the beans for peas, the pepper for corn, the meat for fish. Start by swapping for foods of a similar colour!

Care should be taken that students understand the word 'diet' as eating, not as cutting down and losing weight.

Eating breakfast

Discuss what foods you might have for breakfast, lunch and dinner/tea. *Which is your biggest meal? What do you have?* Do a quick class survey of who eats breakfast and what they have, creating a tally chart on the board.

Things to do

Provide a range of food photographs and/or names of foods on cards for the students to sort. Initially the students could try to put these foods into their own groups and tell you about them. Explain that there are four main groups and how they could alter their groups to make four.

By taking a food from each group the students produce a healthy meal that can be stuck onto a paper plate. These can be displayed on the wall, possibly next to their body cut outs from the previous sessions. Don't forget to include drinks in the discussion, for example fruit juice, water and fizzy drinks.

The food groups at this level would be: meat and fish; vegetables and fruit; potatoes, bread and rice; and fats and sugars. You could limit this to just three food groups if your students struggle with separating 'fats and sugars'. The scientific names for these groups are: proteins; vitamins and minerals; carbohydrates; and fats, respectively. There is a group called 'dairy' but this fits into both protein (eggs) and fats (butter, etc.), which can be confusing.

Differentiation

This works well with real foods or pictures of foods and boxes for the cards to be dropped into. This can create a good class discussion if each student has a single card.

Did you know?

The term 'balanced diet' is hard to explain at this level, but students should grasp that something from every food group or 'box' is required to be healthy.

I wonder...

Water is paramount in our diets. We can live without food for about three weeks, but we can go without water for only three days. *How much water do you drink?* Note that foods contain water too.

Other ideas

- Have an alphabet list ready for compiling a list that has a food, or fruit, or vegetable against each letter – some will be harder than others!

- This could then be used to put messages on the table, by putting out the foods in the order to spell out a word, for example putting out plum, lemon, apple, tomato and egg would spell 'plate'.

- Discuss what is meant by 'junk food' and give some examples. *Is any part of junk food healthy?* Ask why it is junk.

- Ask the students to think of adjectives to describe food, such as chocolate. Go round the class, asking them to give an answer beginning with the letters of the alphabet in order. They might say 'A – amazing', "B – brown', 'C – crunchy', and so on.

Presentation

The students can produce 'healthy plates' of food and attach them to their body and face outlines from the previous lessons.

Plenary

- Share some plates of food or a shopping trolley of your weekly shop and ask the students to swap foods to make the plate or trolley 'healthier'.

- Produce a shopping list for a balanced diet.

Unit 1: Ourselves and other animals – Staying healthy

The objectives for this lesson are that students should be able to:

- State that some foods make them grow and some make them healthy

- Recognize why they should eat more of the healthy foods

- Name some foods that they should eat more of

- Name some foods they should eat less of.

SB p.5   *Starter*

- Share a range of foods as either a colourful image, or a group of foods on a table. Ask the students to choose one that they like best and then to try to explain why they like it. This helps with their articulation and explanation of their ideas.

- Ask the students to pick their favourite type of food. You could limit this to favourite fruits. Create a poem, by writing groups of three foods on the board and then inserting the class favourite between each line, to resemble a poem, e.g.

    Apple, pear, plum
    Grapes
    Grapes, dates, orange
    Grapes
    Pineapple, lemon, pear
    Grapes ...

Explain

Different foods

Students should now be aware that there are different 'groups' of foods. Each group does a different job in the body, but we all need to eat a mixture of them to be healthy.

Show some images of plates of healthy and not so healthy combinations for the students to categorize into these two groups, e.g. fish and chips, salad and meat, curry and rice, fresh fruit salad, chocolate cake etc. Stress that it is not that you can't eat sweets or chips etc, but that you shouldn't eat too much of them and not enough of the other food groups.

How do you grow?

Establish with the students what foods they should eat to grow and which meals they should eat. Traditionally, to be 'healthy' it is said that we should all eat five portions of fruit or vegetables per day. A portion is what you can cup in your hands, so that it is in proportion to your size.

Go through a made up lunch box or school dinner and identify all the fruit and vegetables in there. There may be more than you think. Ask the students how they could get one more portion in, without it being too much to eat, e.g. tomato and lettuce in a sandwich, adding a bunch of grapes, having two vegetables with the hot meal rather than one, etc.

Things to do

Carry out a survey of what foods students eat most of. This could become a rather long list if there are a range of favourite foods, so you could limit it to some main foods, or limit it to a short list of favourite meals. If the information is collected en masse then the students could each colour a square in on a large display sized bar chart for the class to see.

Students often struggle when turning information into bar charts and graphs. Try making a human bar chart to allow them to put themselves in as the data directly. Place pieces of paper with pictures of the main foods on in a line. Ask the students to stand near their favourite one (on the paper). Which is most popular? Then arrange the students into lines rather than groups, to produce the 'human bar chart'. Take a photograph of this from above, if possible and display it in the classroom.

Differentiation

More able students could attempt to colour in squares on a bar chart to represent the photograph then label the favourite food.

Less able students could have a print out of the photograph and label which is the tallest column.

Dig deeper

Many students will already know that if you eat too much fatty food you will become fatter. We all need some fat in our diet, otherwise our bodies don't work properly.

Did you know?

Vitamins and minerals are found in many foods, but mainly in fruit and vegetables. There are more of these in uncooked vegetables and fruit as the cooking process starts to break them down. Also, often when fruit is cooked we add sugar to it. Some vegetables however, need to be cooked otherwise they would be poisonous e.g. potatoes.

I wonder...

We don't continue to grow all our lives, even though we continue to eat.

Other ideas

WS 2

- Start a class record sheet of the different food groups where the students can record the different groups they have eaten each day as a bar chart. Provide a coloured sticker for each group they have eaten each meal time and build it up over a week. Discuss which group is eaten most.

- Use WS 2 to lead the students in a discussion about what types of foods babies, adults and other animals eat. They can then complete the worksheet.

Presentation

Along with the bar charts discussed earlier, the students could produce one sentence to say what their favourite food is and why they think they should eat it. This could be presented to another class or just to each other.

Plenary

Play the 'stations' game. Label places with the main groups of food, e.g. Meat and fish, Vegetables and fruit, Fat. Then place all the students in the middle of the hall/yard. Call out the name of a food and the students have to run to which group they think it belongs to.

A variation would be to have stations called: eat lots, eat some, eat little. Then call out the names of foods. This will assess the students understanding of not only foods and which groups they belong in, but also their understanding of a healthy diet.

Unit 1: Ourselves and other animals – Give me five senses

The objectives for this lesson are that students should be able to:

- Name the five senses

- Understand that sense can be associated with a part of the body

- Take part in 'sense tests' and explain what they see, hear, etc.

- Draw the body parts that relate to the senses.

Starter

SB
p.6

Ask students to sit very still and listen and look around the room. What do they notice? Place some unusual objects around the room, or have something playing music or just ticking, to see if the students can observe these.

Explain

WS
3

The five senses

Explain that our five senses help us understand the world. Using *Student Book* page 6, introduce the senses. *What might you hear, smell, feel, taste and touch during the school day? Which senses can you name? Which part of our body do we use to see, hear, smell, etc.?* Students should point to and name each sense organ.

I spy...

Play the game of 'I spy' to back this up, as it is about what you can see. This game also reinforces the literacy angle of starting letter sounds of words.

Explore in more detail what it is like if you only have one eye to look out of. You lose the sense of depth to your vision and being able to pick things up becomes harder.

This could be adapted to a game of 'I hear'.

Complete WS 3 on page 3 of the *Workbook*.

Things to do

- Play 'Blind man's buff' so that the students can experience what it is like without sight. Ask them to describe what it is like without being able to see.

- Use an eye test chart that has the letters getting gradually smaller. Ask the class to call out the letters that they can see as they get smaller. Discuss how you could make them easier to read. You could make the board go blurry or produce a blurry word on a page and ask the students to try a hand lens and see if this helps or not.

- Listen to a CD of familiar sounds. *How many can you identify?* Make some playing boards illustrating familiar sounds (door slamming, birdsong, bicycle bells, etc.) and use your CD to play sound lotto. The first team to correctly hear, identify and cover all the corresponding pictures on their board wins.

- Play 'What's the time, Mr Wolf?' and discuss whether you can see behind you.

- Play students very quiet music and ask them to say when they can hear the sounds as you turn up the volume. *What happens if you cover up one ear?*

Differentiation

Support less able students to point to their senses in turn. More able students should be encouraged to come up with questions about seeing and hearing that they could test, for example do boys hear better than girls? Do teachers have eyes in the backs of their heads? Do older people see better, or hear better?

Did you know?

If a continual loud noise is played then your ears become 'de-sensitized' and you start to go deaf. If you do this for a long time the deafness will become permanent.

Dig deeper

Blind people have lost their sense of sight but it doesn't mean they cannot 'read'. They use their finger-tips to feel raised bumps (Braille) on a page that they read. They also use talking books to read out loud for them.

I wonder...

Use this question to explore that many people need glasses to improve their eyesight. You can use a magnifying glass to make things bigger and easier to see. You will need to teach students how to use a magnifying glass properly. They should move it steadily between their eye and the object they are viewing to get the bigger/clearest image.

Other ideas

- Discuss what people do who lack one or more senses. You might be able to invite someone with sensory loss to talk about their life and how they compensate.

- Investigate life for students who cannot see or hear. Look at Braille or try to spell names using sign language.

- *How do people who have mobility problems manage?* Explore devices designed to make things easier for the elderly.

Presentation

Let students make up a 'thank-you' poem for their senses and read them out in your next assembly.

Plenary

- *Imagine a world without sounds – what would you miss?*

- Can students point to each of their sense organs? Probe the difference between the sense and its associated organ. *What do I hear with? I use my tongue to ...; I see using my ... .*

- What can you tell from colours of food? Some students expect black to be a blackcurrant taste. Others expect to taste grape.

Unit 1: Ourselves and other animals – I'm sensitive

The objectives for this lesson are that students should be able to:

- Understand how they use their senses and that their senses can help them

- Learn that other animals have the same senses as humans

- Take part in smell or taste tests

- Consider what it would be like to lose their senses.

Starter

SB p.7

- Blindfold some students and ask them to identify objects by their smell, taste or touch alone, for example touch a hard seashell, smell a cut lemon, taste a peppermint sweet.

- Read *The Princess and the Pea* to illustrate that some people are more sensitive than others.

Explain

What's that smell?

Put several smelly objects (e.g. mint, washing powder, grated chocolate, bananas) in foil-covered paper cups. Pierce holes in the foil for the odours to escape. Can students identify the contents just by the smell?

What do nasty smells tell us? Think about 'off' milk and rotten fruit.

Extra sense

Use images of animals' faces to find their eyes and ears. Discuss how they have the same senses as us. Many common animals, like birds and frogs, have no external ears. But their eardrum is on their head surface. They can hear; why else would they make sounds?

Discuss with the students how a person or an animal's face can reveal how they are feeling. The skill of reading facial and body language is a useful social skill for them to develop.

> ⚠ Be alert to food allergies. Do not include nuts or nut products. Ensure clean hands, equipment and surfaces during testing investigations

Things to do

Chop up cubes of fruits and vegetables. Can students identify them blindfolded? Try drops of lemon juice, milkshake, cola and soy sauce on their tongue. *Can you tell them apart if you hold your nose?* Can they identify tastes that are sweet, salty, sour (lemon juice) or bitter (lemon rind)?

Bring in scented gel pens or candles to class. Can students identify the scent? *Is the smell easier to identify if you can see the colour?* Use food colouring to change the colours of common foods (e.g. blue rice).

Differentiation

- For more able students, introduce more complex and unfamiliar tastes, scents and textures. Encourage the use of correct vocabulary: sweet, salty, sour, bitter.

- For less able, reinforce good hygiene and sensible 'turn-taking'. Encourage descriptive language in response to smells and tastes.

Did you know?

Most animals have more sensitive hearing and sight than we do, as they are using them when hunting or being hunted. We are much safer and no long have this need.

Dig deeper

There are other, less well-defined, senses. Among them are a sense of orientation – up and down – and some people talk of a 'sixth sense' that, for example, we are being watched. It is debatable if the sixth sense exists.

I wonder...

This question explores how losing the sense of touch would affect the whole body as we are sensitive all over. Students should think about how they wouldn't be able to pick up fragile objects as they wouldn't feel how delicate they were, or feel hot things or sharp things. They also wouldn't be ticklish.

Other ideas

- Without your sense of smell, your food doesn't taste the same. Try eating a potato and an apple with your nose pinched shut. They taste very similar!

30

- Let students describe objects using as many of their senses as they can (be careful when tasting). Record interesting vocabulary.

- Conduct a favourite/hated taste or smell survey and chart your results. *What are your favourite smells? Which smells don't we like?*

- Tell students about famous people who have achieved greatness despite lacking one or more sense. Mention Beethoven, Helen Keller or Louis Braille. Gary Rhodes the chef doesn't have a sense of smell.

- Read a story or poem about smells.

Presentation

Produce a chart of favourite smells for display.

Students act out how a sense helps us, or act out what it's like not to have the sense.

Plenary

- Ask students: *How do you know that a friend is coming?* or *How do you know what is for dinner? What senses do you use to answer these questions? Which sense do you use most?*

- *Which sense would you like to lose least? Why?*

Unit 1: Ourselves and other animals – Growing older

The objectives for this lesson are that students should be able to:

- Understand that they will change as they get older

- Make observations of similarities and differences in people and animals

- Recognize that humans are animals and that they have similar characteristics to animals and how they grow

- Imagine what might happen if people didn't stop growing.

SB p.8 — Starter

- Ask a parent to bring in a baby. Ask students how they have changed and what they can do now that they couldn't when they were babies.

- Bring in some baby equipment and discuss what it might be for, for example bottles, pouches, nappies, small spoons, clothes, etc. Ask the students whether they need these things now.

Explain

Children find it easier to identify differences rather than similarities. They may not recognize humans, or any animals other than mammals, as animals.

Be alert to the range of family circumstances; handle family likeness in human families with care. Be aware of children living with adoptive parents.

Be prepared for the questions about where babies come from and that you respond in line with your school's policy.

That's not my mummy

Look at pictures of baby animals and corresponding adult animals on *Student Book* page 8. Ask students to match baby to adult.

Use pictures of pairs of animals to match adults and young. Deliberately get it wrong. Can students correct you? *How do you know which goes with which?*

Getting older

Use the images on page 8. How have they changed since they were born? Talk about the similarities and differences between adults and young. Remind students that as we get older we grow bigger – we get heavier and taller.

We don't just change physically. Talk about what the students could do as babies and what they can do now. Make comparisons. For example: 'When I was a baby I couldn't walk; now I can walk and run and jump!'

Ask students to consider what they might be able to do when they are older.

Things to do   WS 4

- Discuss students' own experiences of babies and small children. List what they need to have done for them. *What can you do now? What do you expect to do when you are older that you still can't do?* This could be produced as a table on the board, with three columns: 'baby'; 'now'; 'older'.

- Use picture pair cards to play games such as 'Snap' (match parent to young).

- Encourage the correct terminology for the young of an animal.

- Use WS 4 on page 4 of the *Workbook* and ask students to put the images in order.

Differentiation

More able students could try to match human children to their parents.

Did you know?

Birds are animals that lay eggs. A chicken will recognize its own chicks as it can hear them chirping from inside the egg and the mother will 'talk' back to them. When they hatch (are born) they will have 'imprinted' on each other. This is true of crocodiles and other lizards as well as many other egg-laying animals.

Dig deeper

Discuss if any students have pets at home. Ask: *Did you have them as babies? How have they changed?*

I wonder...

All parts of the body grow up to a point. From about 12 months the head stops growing as fast as the rest of the body. This is why young children appear to have a head much too big for their bodies!

Other ideas

- Ask parents and carers to bring in photographs of the students as babies (ask staff members too) and have a 'Guess the baby' competition.

- Make a 'mobile' of the growing up stages of a human, using images from magazines, or CD-ROMs, or images brought in. Ensure that you have parents' permission to use the images.

Presentation

Encourage 'family' play with baby dolls in your home corner.

Create a display of baby items in a corner of the room.

Create a collage of baby items from pictures and catalogues to display on the wall.

Plenary

- Use pictures from magazines as a sequencing activity to assess knowledge. *Who do you think is older/younger? Why? How tall do you think you will be when you grow up? Why?* Look for evidence of understanding, and where appropriate, evidence from other family members.

- Question students during matching activities to assess understanding. *How are these two alike? What's the same about them? What differences can you see?*

- Make a class thank you letter to any of the visitors that have been into school.

Unit 1: Ourselves and other animals – We all grow

The objectives for this lesson are that students should be able to:

- Compare how humans and animals grow and change

- Make predictions about growing and getting older

- Match animal babies to their correct parents

- Understand that all animals have a life cycle.

SB p.9

Starter

- Show some images of you as a child and discuss how you have changed in appearance from this.

- Use a range of images, either as cards, or on the board, to create the life cycle of a human, showing how we grow older, change, and have more children. You will need to include 'death' as part of this cycle too and be sensitive to this.

- Read a story like *The Very Hungry Caterpillar* and discuss how he changes. This has good links for days of the week, healthy food and for numeracy too.

Explain

We are animals

Most students don't believe that humans are animals. They may think that the words 'animal' and 'mammal' are interchangeable. Make the links between baby humans, baby animals and their parents. This was covered in a previous lesson, but can be reinforced.

Use the image on page 9 of the *Student Book* to discuss how the joey looks like its kangaroo parent and how it needs looking after, and how this is similar to a human.

Discuss what a mother would have to do for her offspring, for example feed it and keep it warm; make a link between humans caring for their baby too.

Invite a parent with a new baby and a toddler to visit.

Whose baby?

The previous lesson looked at matching animal babies that looked like their parents, but in this case the offspring don't look like their parents at first. These pairings are concerned with metamorphic, or bodily change. Use the images on page 9 of the *Student Book* to match the parent and offspring. The maggot may be confused with the caterpillar, so the markings could be discussed.

> ⚠️ All external visits should comply with school guidelines.

Refer to school guidelines for keeping animals in the classroom and apply good hygiene at all times.

Watch out for students with allergies to fur or feathers.

Things to do   WS 5

- Use cut up life cycles of animals and put them in order. Ask the students to tell the story of the butterfly's life cycle, linking it back to *The Very Hungry Caterpillar* story. Develop an understanding that the way some animals move and feed may change as they grow. Ask students to complete WS 5.

- If a tadpole/frogspawn/butterfly/fish tank is set up, discuss the changes the tadpoles/caterpillars/baby fish have gone through.

- Look at the life cycles of mammals in general and link them to humans.

- Ask the students for the names of the offspring of common animals, e.g. kid (goat), puppy (dog). Build up a table of names of offspring to display.

Differentiation

More able students could investigate for how long different animals are dependent on their parents. *Are some animals more dependent on their parents than others? Which ones?*

Did you know?

Caterpillars carry warnings to the other animals that they may be poisonous or unpalatable. A general rule is that orange and black (or yellow/red and black) are warning signs to other animals.

Dig deeper

Fish lay eggs, like birds, but they don't care for their offspring. They lay the eggs in a 'safe' place, then the young (fry) once hatched are on their own.

I wonder...

Elephants and whales have very large babies, as they are a large animal themselves. However, kangaroo and panda babies are very tiny. They are less than 5 cm long at birth. Animals that lay eggs, generally lay eggs that are in proportion to their size.

Other ideas

- This is a great opportunity to visit a farm and investigate animals further.

- Set up a tadpole tank to experience the frog life cycle. Or, set up a caterpillar nursery to experience the butterfly life cycle. Record changes every few days using a digital camera and use the pictures in a wall display or PowerPoint presentation. Students could sequence them too.

- Create a timeline of a human life.

Presentation

Produce a drama to illustrate the life cycle of the frog or the butterfly. You could get the students to act out the story of *The Very Hungry Caterpillar*.

Produce a booklet of the life cycle of a frog or whichever animal you have observed in your tank.

Plenary

- Place the following words on the board and discuss if they are something that humans do and if other animals do it – producing two groups of words, for example: feed; keep warm; care for; protect; grow; change.

- Read *The Very Hungry Caterpillar* again and ask students to describe in their own words how the animal changes as it gets older.

- Produce your own version with the students of *The Very Hungry Caterpillar*, but about a tadpole.

Unit 1: Ourselves and other animals – Unit 1 Review

The objectives for this lesson are that students should be able to:

- Check what they have learned about themselves and other animals in this unit

- Find out how they are working towards, within and beyond the Grade 1 level.

SB p.10 *Expectations*

Note: *items in italic are this Unit's scientific enquiry expectations.*

At the end of this Unit students working towards Grade 1 level will:

- identify and locate parts of their body

- use their observations to describe humans and other animals

- *begin to make comparisons.*

In addition, students working within Grade 1 level will:

- identify and their sense organs

- recognize changes that take place as animals get older

- compare humans to other animals

- recognize the need for a healthy diet

- *communicate observations and measurements*

- *use their observations to compare differences between humans and other animals.*

Further to this, students working beyond Grade 1 level will also:

- explain differences between living and non-living things in terms of characteristics such as movement and growth

- explain that adult animals no longer grow

- describe how animals other than humans grow and change

- *communicate ideas*

- *make observations about other animals*

- *suggest ways of presenting observations.*

Check-up

The 'humans are animals' issue crops up time and again. This would be a good point at which to compare all the things we know about animals and their systems, such as eating, growing up, having babies, moving, breathing, to show that we are the same.

Assessment WS 6

Use the Unit 1 assessment to check the students' understanding of the content of the unit. The answers are given below.

Name: _____ Date: _____

WS 6

Unit 1 Assessment

1 My five senses are _____

2 Safia has a pet rabbit.

What must the rabbit have to live? Tick (✓) them.

3 Join the baby animal to its parent with a line.

4 Circle the things that are alive.

6 Heinemann Explore Science Grade 1

Written assessment

Answers to Workbook WS 6, Unit 1 review

1 Sight, hearing, smell, taste, touch.
Could accept eyes, ears, nose, mouth/tongue, hand.

2 Food, water.

3 Kitten → cat; duckling → duck; lamb → sheep.

4 Child, snail, plant.

The answer!

How can you tell who someone is without using your eyes? (see page 1, Student Book)

There are many ways to recognize who someone is, including smell, touch and listening just to their breathing. The more you close your eyes the more sensitive your other senses become.

And finally...

- Displaying a really tall figure of a giant on a high wall provides a striking background for displayed work on growth and change.

- Display pictures of the school staff when young to match with their current photos.

- Produce a movable display with images of life cycles of the frog, butterfly and human on Velcro so that students can move them around. Add some words for the stages of the cycles to be added in the right places. Discuss how each cycle is different from ours.

New International Edition

Unit 2: Growing plants

The objectives for this Unit are that students should be able to:

- Know that plants are living things

- Know that some things have never been alive

- Know that different plants and animals inhabit local environments

- Understand what a plant is and name the major parts of plants

- Know that plants need light and water to grow

- Make observations of plants and seeds

- Record what they have discovered during investigations.

SB pp.11–20 *Science background*

An amazing diversity of plant life exists, even in the most unpromising of locations. To survive, each plant species needs suitable growing conditions. In this Unit we encourage students to discover the conditions plants need for healthy growth.

Although students may have had the opportunity to grow cress seeds or other quick-growing seeds in nursery or reception classes, this may be the first time they have looked at plant growth in detail. Observing plants around them will give students a perspective on their local environment and encourage sensitivity towards it.

This Unit introduces students to the idea of plants as living things that grow and change. Encourage students to look carefully at plants and seeds and describe what they see.

The importance of plants

A world without plants would be a barren place. Without plants there can be no land animals and certainly no humans! Green plants are the key to almost all life on Earth, transforming energy from the Sun into food for us and for other animals. Few living things can survive without oxygen. Green plants take in carbon dioxide and release oxygen into the atmosphere, constantly renewing it. We use plants for food, drink, cosmetics and medicines. We decorate our homes with them, process them into newspapers and clothes, carve them into furniture and even smear plant products on our skin. Encourage your students to recognize the huge role that plants play in our lives and to take care of the plants in their environment.

What is a plant?

Children may have a very narrow understanding of what a plant is. Some believe that a plant is something cultivated, which rules out 'weeds', and grass, too. Others may think that the plants we eat are not 'plants' but 'vegetables' or 'fruit', which they consider to be something entirely different. In fact, trees, grass, weeds, fruit and vegetables are all plants or parts of them and share similarities. Children find it easier to identify differences, so help them to find similarities and things that all plants have in common. Encourage them to stretch their descriptive vocabulary, and their use of comparative language such as taller than, wider than, and thinner than.

Parts of plants

Students at this level need to recognize and be able to name the main plant parts, which are:

Roots: these anchor the plant to the soil and draw water and tiny amounts of dissolved minerals from the soil to the rest of the plant. There are two main types of root: tap-roots (e.g. carrot roots, which are long, thick and straight), and fibrous roots that have many offshoots. Both have lots of root hairs. The purpose of the root hairs is to increase the surface area of the roots in contact with the damp soil and so make uptake of water more efficient.

Leaves: these are the food 'factories' of the plant. They collect energy from the Sun and combine water and carbon dioxide into sugars for the plant to use. This process is called photosynthesis. The larger the surface area of the leaf, the more efficient it is at collecting sunlight. Plants' leaves are generally arranged so that no leaf will overlap or shade another.

Stem: this keeps the plant upright, holding the leaves towards the Sun. The stem moves water from the roots to other parts of the plant. The trunk of a tree is a large woody stem.

Flower: this is the reproductive part of a plant where fruit and seeds form. Not all plants have visible flowers or ones that are brightly coloured.

Requirements for plant growth

Plants grow using the food they make themselves through photosynthesis. If a plant cannot photosynthesize (make food) it will die. Although a plant may continue to grow without light it is using its food reserves to do so and cannot keep growing indefinitely. Plants grown in the dark will be etiolated – thin, yellow, weak and straggly – indicating that the plant is growing long in search of light.

To photosynthesize, a plant needs light, water, the correct temperature and carbon dioxide. At this level we focus on a plant's need for light and water. Deprived of either one of these, a plant will eventually die.

Students need to understand that light can come from the Sun as well as other sources. Including cacti in the range of plants students explore serves a number of purposes: their exotic nature can challenge typical concepts of what a plant is, and they promote students' understanding that plants grow best in conditions which are most appropriate to their needs.

Help students to understand that a plant grows by adding to itself, increasing the number of leaves and branches, not by just 'getting bigger', like blowing up a balloon.

This Unit gives students several opportunities to undertake investigations and turn their ideas into forms that can be tested. They will also have the chance to:

- make detailed observations
- make and record measurements
- use the results of their experimenting to draw conclusions.

In *Thirsty plants* and *Give me sunshine* (pages 50–53, *Student Book* pages 16–17) students learn about the conditions needed for healthy plant growth. In *Seeds inside* (page 54, *Student Book* page 19) students plant bean seeds to watch them grow.

Language

Alive Being able to grow, have young and change when their environment changes.

Bar chart A graph, where the length of each bar stands for a separate piece of data.

*****Dehydrate** To lose water.

*****Etiolation** Rapid lengthening of the stem of a plant accompanied by small, underdeveloped leaves and yellow colouring; all due to lack of light.

Flower The part of a flowering plant from which the fruit or seed is developed.

Fruit The enlarged ovary of a flowering plant where the seeds are contained.

*****Germinate** When a seed starts to grow.

Grow To get bigger by adding to yourself.

Leaf The main food-producing part of a plant.

Petals Parts of a flower (often brightly coloured) that protect the flower's reproductive organs and may help attract pollinators, like insects, to the flower.

*****Photosynthesis** The way a plant makes its own food and nutrients using sunlight, carbon dioxide and water.

Pictogram A graph, where each picture represents a separate piece of data.

Root The part of a plant under the ground that takes in water.

Sap A liquid containing water, minerals and food that moves through the plant.

Seed The thing a plant grows from, containing its own food supply, usually with a protective coating.

Seedling A young plant grown from seed.

*****Sepal** The part of a plant that protects the petals when the flower is still in bud.

Stem The part of the plant that supports its leaves and flowers and transports water, minerals and food.

Veins Tubes in a leaf through which sap flows.

Wilt To become limp.

* Technical definitions generally for teachers, not students, at this stage.

Key vocabulary

The following words might be introduced or used with the children alongside others, to accustom them to the nature of scientific vocabulary:

communicate	observe
compare	predict
contrast	record
describe	similar to
different from	test (ideas)
like (comparison)	

39

These words may be of use in terms of comparisons:

bark	**not alive**
branch	**plant (noun/verb)**
dead	**tall/taller/tallest**
healthy	**water (noun/verb)**
light	**weed**
living	**wilt**

Resources

A full list of resources is located at the end of the Introduction to this Guide, for ease of gathering resources. Many resources will already be in the classroom, but a few may need prior arrangement. For example:

- A selection of potted plants – various types and sizes, including a pot-bound plant, a tomato plant and cacti leaves, and a large cabbage (red or green).

- Plaster of Paris.

- Gardening tools, seed catalogues and packets of seeds – flowers and vegetables.

- A selection of quick-growing seeds to germinate, e.g. cress, sunflower, nasturtium, radish.

- A selection of bean seeds, e.g. broad beans, mung beans.

- A selection of fruit seeds, like pumpkin or melon.

- Some bulbs, e.g. hyacinth, onion.

- A selection of seeds and seed casings, e.g. coconuts, poppies, pine-cones, bird seed, vegetables (cauliflower, broccoli, celery, spinach).

- An artificial flower and an artificial plant.

- The reader *Growing Plants* may be used with this Unit. Students do not need to know names, but do emphasize the variety of shapes, sizes and colours of plants.

Bright ideas

- Go on a plant walk and spot as many plants as possible.

- Collect leaves to make pictures.

- Other investigations that you might like to try are:

  What conditions do seeds need to germinate?

  Are all plants the same, wherever they grow?

  Are the tallest plants the ones with the most leaves?

  Do the biggest flowers have the most petals?

  Do the biggest seeds produce the biggest plants? (Conversely, do the biggest plants produce the biggest seeds?)

Knowledge check

From Unit 1 students will have learned that humans and animals are alive and that they grow by adding to themselves. Now we will extend this knowledge to plants.

This is the introductory Unit for plants but most students should be able to identify one or two examples of 'a plant' in their immediate environment. Students may have a vocabulary of descriptive words relating to plants (colour, size) but this should not be assumed. Many students may recognize some of the words relating to parts of plants but many may not.

Skills check

Students need to:

- be encouraged to observe (look closely at) their plants and seeds.

- to use a hand lens or magnifying glass where appropriate.

- be supported to record what they see and what they have discovered.

This is an opportunity to develop descriptive and comparative language – taller than, shorter than, round, jagged, smooth, hairy, etc.

Links to other subjects

Literacy: Read stories and poems about plants, seeds and animals growing. Write a story about a magic plant or seed. Read and use captions and labels. Write captions and labels for their own work. Follow simple instructions, including recipes that use plants. Make simple lists and write simple instructions. Develop your home corner into a role-play garden centre to develop language about plants. Students could develop drama skills by acting out a story about a plant.

Numeracy: Opportunities for counting up to, and beyond, ten. Read, write and order numbers. Make comparisons of height and compare numbers of leaves or petals. Measure volumes of water in non-standard units. Opportunities to measure time in days and weeks and use calendars as recording devices. Talk about the shapes we see in plants. *What shape are the petals? If we cut across the stem what shape is it?*

Art and design: Students can draw, paint or sculpt plants, make prints and casts from leaves or bark, press flowers and use seeds, twigs and bark as collage materials. Over several centuries, painters have created many styles of still life paintings with fruits, vegetables and plants. Show some to the students; talk about them and let them create their own versions. There are many design and technology possibilities using plants and plant parts as decorations. Consider also using plant-based fabric dyes as part of a design and technology project.

ICT: In ICT use a digital camera to record work. Encourage students to use a word processing program to write labels for their experiments. Use a paint program to draw plants and flowers; show students how to change the brush, colours and line thickness to create their imaginary plant.

Let's find out...

This Unit opens with this question:

Why do we call some plants weeds?

This question helps to clarify that weeds are plants. They are normally thrown away or removed from the garden, so may not be considered as 'living'.

Unit 2: Growing plants – Dead or alive?

The objectives for this lesson are that students should be ale to:

- Understand whether or not a plant is alive

- Explain simple differences between artificial and living plants

- Consider whether objects are alive, not alive or were once alive

- Grow seeds into plants and observe the changes.

SB p.12 | Starter

- Make a class KWL grid (showing what they already **K**now about plants, **W**ant to know or check, and finally what they have **L**earned) to refer to throughout the topic.

- Bring in a dead or dying plant and a similar artificial plant. Say: 'I just don't know what has gone wrong. I put both of the plants on my windowsill and treated them both the same but look … .' Can students tell you why the plants have reacted differently? Prompt them to discuss how to classify something as being 'alive' or not.

Explain

Some students have difficulty understanding that trees, cacti, grass and moss are all plants. Some students may need help understanding that pictures 'represent' plants in the 'plant or pretender' activity.

The starter activity links straight into page 12 of the *Student Book*. The students need to decide what the criteria are for something being alive. Use the acronym 'MR GREEN' – **M**ovement; **R**eproduction; **G**rowth; **R**espiration; **E**xcretion; **E**xcitability; **N**utrition. There are various forms of this acronym but all spell out the same seven life processes. The students don't need to know all seven life processes or their terms, but should have a general list for classification.

⚠️ Students must wash their hands after handling seeds or soil.

Things to do

- Start to grow small seeds likes cress. Take photographs of their development over the next week.

- Discuss whether the seed is alive. Although seeds don't exhibit the seven life processes at once; they are 'dormant' or waiting for the right time to germinate when they have the best conditions for growing into a healthy plant.

- *Can we make a dead plant come alive again?* What do the students think? Explain that eventually all plants die.

- Play 'Dead or alive' to clarify a plant or other object being alive or not. Label one side of the room 'alive', the other side 'not alive'. Label the front of the class 'never alive'. Show students photographs or pictures of various plants, including trees, Venus fly-traps, cacti, grass, seaweed and moss, stones, hills, birds, humans, plastic plants, wax dummies, cars, etc. Give some students an actual photo/plant/object each. They then take turns to move pictures/plants/objects to one side or the other, explaining why they've chosen that side. Do the class agree or disagree? All correct answers score a point and they could play in teams. After each turn talk about why something is alive or not.

Differentiation

As additional work for some groups, you can ask them to compare dried flowers to living ones and decide if they were alive or not.

Did you know?

The germinating seed activity should illustrate this point.

Dig deeper

If you put the seeds in a warmer place they should germinate faster. If they don't have much light once germinated, they will grow tall, but pale and spindly. Many students won't recognize this as being unhealthy though.

I wonder...

Show students a cut flower and a similar artificial flower (or green plant). *Are they the same? What is the same/different about them? Are they alive?*

How do we know? What if we planted the real and artificial flowers – which would grow?

Other ideas

- What curious trees can they imagine? A chocolate tree, a shoe tree, a candyfloss tree? Ask them to paint their tree.

- Make a 'garden centre' role-play area with seeds, plants, flowers, tools, seed catalogues and gardening magazines.

Presentation

Use your 'Dead or alive' pictures and objects to sort into a Venn diagram using PE hoops.

Press flower petals and make into images or put between clear plastic film in patterns on the windows. Discuss whether these are alive, dead or never alive.

Plenary

- Go back to the plastic plants and dead plant and introduce a stuffed toy animal. Discuss whether they are alive or not, or whether they have died. What criteria would you have to tell if something had never lived? This could include things like: not made of something 'natural' or that it doesn't have a mouth.

43

Unit 2: Growing plants – Plenty of plants

The objectives for this lesson are that students should be able to:

- Find out where different plants grow

- Make simple observations of their world that they can record

- Recognize and name some plants

- Understand that some animals eat plants.

SB p.13   *Starter*

- Discuss what we wouldn't have if we didn't have any plants. Emphasize that it isn't just gardens. Show images of animals, including humans eating plants. Show birds nesting in trees and lily pads with frogs on them and fish sheltering under them. What do we need plants for?

Explain

Students may not identify trees or grasses as plants.

I live here

The walk around the grounds (in 'things to do') will help students to notice that the same plant doesn't grow in all places. Look at plants in open sunny areas and in shady areas.

Me too!

Animals also live in a variety of places, but by looking at contrasting environments the students should notice different plants and different animals. At this stage, this is sufficient. Encourage students to explore and talk about what they observe.

> ⚠ Watch for possible plant allergies and avoid getting sap on skin. Students must wash their hands after handling plants or soil.

Things to do

- Go on a walk around the school grounds, looking for as many plants as you can. Ask students to record as many different plants as possible – use a digital camera. When back in school, mark on a large map on the board where most of the plants were found; for example not in the yard, but on the field. If you don't have grounds or a field, go for a walk in your local environment. Discuss why you should not damage or pull out plants.

- Name some of the more common plants that were seen.

- Go on a plant treasure hunt to find only certain colours of flower/plant or long leaves.

- Make a 'plant palette' – carefully stick small parts of different plants (e.g. leaves, flowers, seed-heads) onto a card artist's palette covered with double-sided sticky tape. Discuss the variety of shapes and colours. *How many different shades of green can we find? Would we find more plants in the spring, summer, autumn or winter? Why?*

- Explain that there is a huge variety of shapes and sizes of plant; some plants are not obvious. *Are trees plants? What about moss or grass?* Make a map of your school grounds showing the location of various plants – in flowerbeds, on the field, in wall cracks, etc.

Differentiation

More able students could describe some of the plants they found. Encourage descriptive vocabulary and list interesting words.

Did you know?

Generally animals eat plants as they are at the start of the 'food chain'. However carnivorous plants have evolved to take advantage of the very nutrient rich source of food that an insect can offer. Most other plants get these nutrients from the decayed remains of dead animals that are in the soil. Students don't need to know about 'food chains' at this point.

Dig deeper

Grass and trees are also part of the plant kingdom. Unlike other flowering plants, their wind-pollinated flowers may not be brightly coloured.

I wonder...

Plant-like organisms grow in snow, but these are related to mosses and algae. There aren't any nutrients in snow and the cold prevents 'real' plants from growing.

There are plants in the desert, which have adapted to very little water.

Other ideas

- Make a rubbing of tree bark or make a Plasticine mould of bark to be cast in Plaster of Paris.

- Gather flowers and leaves from plants from your walk and sort them into groups, or stick them onto a map of the area you walked. Add images of the animals that could live there.

Presentation

Using wax crayons, make leaf rubbings, or leaf prints using paint. Cut out finished leaves and make a class 'beanstalk' for display.

Sandwich leaves or flowers between sheets of clear sticky-backed plastic, frame and mount on windows to show the variety of plants found outside.

Plenary

- Provide images of common plants and ask for their names, for example grass, tree, some of the flowers etc.

- Match the photographs of the areas of your walk to some plants found there.

45

Unit 2: Growing plants – Plant parts

The objectives for this lesson are that students should be able to:

- Name some of the different parts of a plant

- Compare different plants, pointing out similarities and differences

- Draw and label a plant, including its roots

- Make models of an imaginary plant.

SB p.14

Starter

- Use a series of cut-up plant parts as a jigsaw to make up a real plant on the board. Discuss what they might be called.

- Make some observational drawings of flowers and leaves, to focus on colour and shape.

- Use enlarged images of parts of plants very close up, asking the students to say what they think they are as you pan out, so the object becomes more recognizable as they see the whole picture.

Explain

What am I?

Make observational drawings of a range of plants and label the parts that they can see. Some students may be able to come up with sophisticated labels, for example bud, twig, petals, which are provided on *Student Book* page 14.

Ask students to describe the part without saying its name as a guessing game. For example, 'I am green, long and thin with something pretty at the end. What am I?' (Stem).

Develop the understanding that, although the plants are different, they do share common features.

What's underneath?

Discuss which parts of a plant are under the soil. Ask students to make predictions about this and draw what they think. Take a plant out of its pot, or take the students outside to dig one up from the ground. Use hand lenses to observe roots closely. What do they notice? They will observe fine root hairs.

Things to do

- Give students a cauliflower or head of calabrese/broccoli, a stem of celery, some spinach leaves and some carrots or parsnip roots and ask them (without naming the components) to assemble an imaginary plant.

- Can they then label it? What other vegetables and other plants do they need to finish it off?

- Photograph their models and display them.

Differentiation

Ask more able students to prepare a plant or flower book. Common flowers could be pressed, dried and identified. Extend vocabulary to: vein, petal, sepal, bud, shoot, if appropriate.

Share some more unusual plants with more able students. Discuss if they have the same parts.

Did you know?

Cacti don't have 'true' leaves. They have developed very tiny spines to reduce water loss in the hot conditions of the desert.

Dig deeper

Some students may already know what petals, thorns and bulbs are. Discuss with them and share some examples in real life.

I wonder...

Not all plant stems and leaves are green. Some are red, white, purple or even brown; even when it is the height of the growing season. For example, Copper beech, purple Heucheras, red-leaved Acers, and rhubarb all have reddish coloured leaves.

Other ideas

- Play 'Pass the cabbage': each student unwraps a leaf from a cabbage (or lettuce). Hold the leaf up to the light – *what do you see?* Veins.

- Cut a red cabbage in half to show the leaves and pattern inside.

- Grow your own tomato plants. You can buy seeds, or collect seed from mature tomatoes. Discuss how the plant grows. It does not draw its food from the soil, nor from fertilizer, although this may be called 'tomato feed'.

- If possible, take the students to a garden centre to observe the range of plants there. Ask them to point out the parts on plants they see. Set them the challenge to find a plant with certain coloured leaves, or stems. Can they find them? What is the most usual colour?

Presentation

Make picture cards for a locally-found plant species. Include identification tips: the number of petals, its shape, colour and texture of leaves, thickness of stem, etc. *Do all plants have visible flowers? Do all plants have the same roots?*

Plenary

- To check whether students can name and identify the main parts of a plant, ask them to draw and label a flowering plant, including what they know is under the ground.

47

Unit 2: Growing plants – Leaves and roots

The objectives for this lesson are that students should be able to:

- State that plants need water and light

- Recognize that plants use these to grow

- Recognize the part of a plant that takes in water.

SB p.15 — Starter

- Bring in a selection of fruits and vegetables. Ask: 'Why do we grow plants?' Look at apples, carrots, potatoes, celery, rhubarb, leeks and peas. Ask: 'Which parts of the plant are these?'; 'Have you ever tasted these plants?' Separate out root vegetables. Explain that these special roots are eaten by humans (and some animals) as food.

- Read the story of the Enormous Turnip and discuss why they could not pull it out.

Explain

Some students may think that roots are what plants grow from, because it is the part in the soil.

What do roots do?

Look at *Student Book* page 15 and encourage students to identify as many roots as possible. Ask: *What do we use these roots for? What plants do they come from?* You could link this with previous activities of eating fruit and vegetables and record the roots eaten over a week.

Show the students a pot plant. *Can you remember what the parts of the plant are called? Are there any parts we can't see?* Take the plant out of its pot then examine and describe the root structure. *What are the roots for?*

The activity explores more about what roots do in terms of drawing water from the soil.

What is a leaf for?

Plants use their leaves for photosynthesis – a chemical reaction in the cells of the leaf that turns water, carbon dioxide and energy from light into oxygen and sugars and starches for growth.

Students at this level don't need to know this detail, but they should be aware that a leaf uses light. The challenge later in the Unit helps with this.

Show a range of leaves that we eat and discuss what plants they are from.

> ⚠ Some plants are poisonous to us – we can't eat everything! Ensure good hygiene when handling or eating plants. Watch out for food allergies.

Things to do

- Ask the students what they think will happen to a plant without roots? What happens to plants when their roots don't have room to grow? Compare a pot-bound plant with one that has room for the roots to grow. Ask: 'Which plant looks healthiest?'

- Compare the roots of an established plant and a seedling. Note the differences and establish that roots grow. Discuss how roots can be different shapes, sizes and colours.

- You can grow seedlings in the clear jelly, or even just in water. Do this in small, clear, plastic cups or beakers, so that the roots can be observed regularly.

- Give students cups of water and a straw each. Drink through the straw – this is like what the root does. Mention that another job roots have is to hold the plant in the ground.

- Follow a recipe for root vegetable soup and enjoy!

- Outside, look for tree roots that have come above ground. Ask: 'Do big plants have big roots?' If you have sunflowers, look at the base that grows out at an angle (buttress roots). Ask: 'Why does a tall plant need them?'

- Take a small plant and remove all its leaves. Observe whether it grows or dies. You could remove varying numbers of leaves from different plants, or just remove the leaves from some seedlings if you don't want to destroy a whole plant!

- Share a plant that has not been watered, and one that has, as well as one that has grown in the dark. What do they think is wrong with each plant?

Differentiation

Introduce more unfamiliar roots/foods, for example sweet potato, beetroot, ginger. Ask students to use books to identify them and explain their uses and purpose.

Did you know?

The *Victoria Amazonica* lily can grow leaves up to over 2.5 m in diameter. These are often shown in photographs with a small child sat in the middle of them. They can support more weight than this if it is evenly distributed! They grow so big to get as much light as possible and to stop other plants from getting the light too – a way of reducing the competition.

Dig deeper

Humans use plants for making fabrics, medicines, food, dyes and perfumes.

Discuss other plant products we use, for example cotton, rubber, medicines, paper and card. Add these unusual plant products to your plant display (in a separate list) and discuss how important plants are to us.

I wonder...

You can eat some flowers, for example nasturtium flowers in salads! Discuss what other parts of a plant we eat, for example stems, roots, leaves, seeds.

Other ideas

- Grow hyacinth or onion bulbs without soil by resting in a jar of water; dip the roots in water and watch the growth.

- Make a collection of simple vegetable recipes.

Presentation

Use fruits and vegetables in still life painting. Show students examples by Cezanne and Giovanna Garzoni. Let them create their own versions of these paintings.

Make prints using potatoes or other root vegetables of fruits (apples and peppers work well).

Plenary

- Prepare examples of unfamiliar, interesting or exotic fruits and vegetables to taste. Which parts of plants are they from?

- Cut a large picture of a plant into pieces – flower, stem, roots and leaves. Invite students to name the parts and put them in the right places. Talk about the features of the different parts. Can students identify them on plants in school?

New International Edition

Unit 2: Growing plants – Thirsty plants

The objectives for this lesson are that students should be able to:

- Understand that plants need water to survive and grow

- Find out what happens to plants that aren't watered

- Measure volumes of water to give to plants

- Present their results in writing or drawing form.

SB p.16   Starter

- Display some wilted plants or seedlings. *What could be wrong with these plants?* If necessary, prompt by asking students to feel how dry the soil is. *Do plants need water to grow?* Encourage students to think of ways of finding out. Ask what they expect to happen to plants that are deprived of water.

- *How do we feel when we are thirsty?* Talk about dehydration and how important it is for people and other living things to have enough water. Discuss drought and its effects on crops in developing countries.

The challenge

Discuss what students think will happen to the plants that aren't watered.

Model pouring the water in very badly without bothering to measure it. Discuss if this would be a good way to find out. Students make suggestions and, as a class, decide what to do. Students then follow instructions.

What to do

Encourage practical skills, for example measuring a volume of water in different containers, using standard and non-standard measures to record plant growth.

The two plants will need to be fairly 'dry' beforehand to ensure that the results don't take too long to produce.

Each group of students can have two plants to set up if space allows so the groups' results can be compared. Did all the watered plants survive?

What you need

- Cups or jugs.

- Sweet basil works well for instant results. However, you may want to use something that produces results over time, for example geraniums, but be conscious that the students may lose interest if the activity is too long.

What to check

Students will need help with measuring and carefully pouring, particularly those with less fine motor skills.

Ensure that the students don't water both pots!

Ensure that the students are following the instructions carefully.

They need to observe the plants carefully.

> ⚠️ Students must wash their hands after handling seeds or soil.

Differentiation

For groups who work fast and have good investigation skills, you can ask them to measure how much water they give using an empty film canister. Give one just one a day; another one two, etc. Notice that you can over-water. More is not always better!

What did you find?

Look again at pages 15–16 of the *Student Book* and talk about how important water is for plants and all living things. Reinforce the idea that to be healthy plants need water.

Discuss whether the amount of water is important.

Record

Help students record their observations in pictures or words and talk about what their pictures show. (This should be ongoing for as long as the experiment is in progress.)

Did you know?

Show examples of cacti. These are special plants that can live in very dry places; they don't need very much water to survive.

Cacti and succulents store water inside themselves. Cacti do this in their stems, succulent plants do this in their leaves, others in pitchers, like the pitcher plant, and some in their roots as tubers. People in hot dry places may dig up the tubers to extract the water from them.

Plenary

- Discuss points that help clarify the need for watering plants, such as what happens to grass (goes brown) in hot summers, but flowers like dandelions stay green. *Which has the longer root? Which can reach the water deep in the soil?* To show what is happening, soak some dehydrated food, for example dried mushrooms, onions or chillies.

- Make up a rhyme to say how gardens grow. Write the rhyme. Or write a letter to a friend to tell them how gardens grow.

New International Edition

Unit 2: Growing plants – Give me sunshine

The objectives for this lesson are that students should be able to:

- Understand that plants need light to grow
- Compare green plants grown in light and dark places
- Observe and record the changes in each plant
- Share and discuss what they discover.

SB pp.17–18   Starter

- Recap that you know plants need water to grow by bringing in a growing pot of the herb sweet basil that has been left unwatered for two or three days. Discuss how we can 'revive it'. Watered, it will revive noticeably in a matter of hours. Also have a plant that has been left too long. Try the same thing. *Would this work for all plants?*

- *What else might plants need to grow well?* Prompt students to say where the growing plants were placed (in the Sun), if necessary.

- Put a healthy pot plant in a dark cupboard for a week or two – *what happens to the leaves?* Discuss how this plant is like the girls' grass on page 17.

- *Is it possible to give a plant too much water, or expose it to too much sunlight?*

The challenge

Read the conversation between Sheila and Habiba on page 17 of the *Student Book*.

Sheila and Habiba need to test if it is water or light that caused the grass to go yellow. Encourage students to think about what they have already discovered about plants needing water from the previous experiment. Who do they think is right?

What to do   WS 7

How could we test that plants need light to grow? Brainstorm all ideas and let students devise their own investigations. Ask what the students predict will happen to plants deprived of light.

Extend questioning on setting up an investigation. Let students explain what they are doing and why. *Why do the girls need to water the grass first?* Give each group a tray of healthy, newly-germinated plants such as salad cress. Cover an

area with a black paper cone to block out the light. Place on a sunny windowsill and water as normal. Look at the plants regularly. *What do you notice?* Encourage use of comparative language. Help students record their observations in pictures or words. *What do your pictures show?* (This will be ongoing over the next week or two.)

What you need

- Opaque plastic sheet or other covering material.
- Two trays of seedlings already germinated and about 1 cm tall.
- A small watering can.

What to check

Ensure that the students are clear that the plants still need water and so must be watered every day.

Ensure that the students don't leave the covering off the tray of seedlings.

> ⚠ Students must wash their hands after handling seeds or soil.

Differentiation

Give more able students a greater role in planning the investigation. Ask them to look for ways of making it fair. For example, using identical plants.

Can the students come up with any new ways of measuring growth? (Number of leaves, thickness of stem, etc.)

Can they increase the rate of growth using a mini-greenhouse, i.e. alter the temperature?

What did you find?

Look at page 18 of the *Student Book* and comment on the images that the girls have drawn. *Are they like the ones we have recorded? Do the taller plants look healthier? Why have they grown taller?*

Without light, plants grow long and spindly. Students often believe that the light-deprived plant has grown more or is a better grower. Talk about how healthy the plants are.

Record

Record the changes daily with a digital camera and use these on the board to sequence the seedlings growth.

Students draw their observations or talk to a partner every day.

You could cover an area of grass with a piece of black plastic or an old carpet tile to block out the sunlight. The grass underneath should become yellow, then green again when uncovered.

Did you know?

Although plants will survive with water and light, the Sun also provides heat. Plants don't grow very well when cold. Some become dormant. Some die. Plants grow faster and bigger in warmer (but not too warm) conditions.

Plenary

WS 8

- WS 8 could help record the learning.

- Remind students of the visit to the garden centre (if you carried it out) and ask them to produce a plant label for caring for a plant, for example how it needs light and water.

Unit 2: Growing plants – Seeds inside

The objectives for this lesson are that students should be able to:

- Understand that plants grow from seeds

- Predict how a seed will grow

- Observe and explore how plants grow

- Make daily records of their observations in charts.

SB p.19

Starter

- Read the story of *Jack and the Beanstalk*. Why did his beans grow?

- Discuss ideas about how plants grow.

- *What do we mean by 'grow'?* (Refer back to Unit 1 – what do students remember about human and animal growth?)

- Show students one large and one small plant of the same type. In time, the smaller plant will grow to be the same as the larger one. What differences can they spot? (Height, number of leaves, thickness of stem, size of leaves.)

Explain

Make sure you plant several 'spares' – some seeds may not germinate and students will be disappointed.

Is my plant alive?

This reinforces that plants are alive and that sometimes we can 'revive' them with water. The seed will grow if watered. This is an opportunity to set up a range of large seeds, for the 'Things to do' section.

Which comes first?

The root comes first in search of water. The shoot unfurls from the seed to search for light.

> ⚠ Some seeds are coated in fungicides or pesticides and should be avoided. Beware of poisonous plants.
>
> Students must wash their hands after handling seeds or soil.

Things to do

- Set up large bean seeds in jam jars so that the root and shoot can be observed. (Bean seeds will germinate faster if they are soaked for 24 hours first.) Encourage students to either photograph these or to draw their growth every two days.(Preparation is key here – have some that are just starting to germinate that you can 'swap' for the students' ones, so that they aren't waiting for the seeds to start for a week before they can record.)

- Ask students to predict how the seed will grow – record in a concertina book. Students could even take digital photos of their bean's progress to stick in their books.

- Measure heights of plants daily and record on individual and class charts, either in block graphs or pictorially.

- Using a digital camera, record the growth of a 'class plant' every day. Display the pictures around the room as a frieze.

- Cut open fruits to find seeds (e.g. pumpkins and melons).

Differentiation

Encourage more able students to ask their own questions about plant growth, for example: *Will plants grow in a fridge? Will plants grow if watered with lemonade?* and to devise ways to answer them.

Let students design their own seed packet including instructions – have they included information on giving their plants enough light and water?

Did you know?

Let a bean seedling find its way to the sunlight in a plant maze. Cut a small hole in the top of a shoebox. Put the bean plant inside and insert card barriers for the bean to negotiate as it seeks the light.

Do a similar experiment with a sprouting potato.

Dig deeper

The seeds on a strawberry are on the outside rather than the inside of the fruit!

I wonder...

Seeds germinate in moist, warm conditions.

Other ideas

- Use secondary sources to compile an 'interesting facts' chart about plants and seeds – largest, smallest, most poisonous, etc.

- Plant a variety of fruit and vegetable seeds in a window garden.

- Make a miniature salad garden using fast-growing seeds, like mung beans, alfalfa, cress and radish.

- Paint faces on eggshell 'flowerpots', fill with damp cotton wool or compost and sow cress or grass seed to create living 'hair'.

Presentation

Make a picture frame from card and decorate with a pattern of seeds. 'Varnish' it when dry using PVA glue.

Make a seed collage picture.

Plenary

WS 9

- Discuss what a seed needs to grow and, together, write the instructions for the back of a seed packet. By comparing existing instructions, establish that some plants need more/less light/warmth/water than others. Draw together all you have learned about the need for water and light.

- Students can play the game on WS 9.

- Bring in a tomato plant, a few seeds and a tomato. Ask a student to help you put them in growth order. *But that's funny! What comes before this seed, then? And what comes after this tomato? So where does it stop? Oh, it doesn't! Tell me more.*

- *What would happen if plants never stopped growing?*

New International Edition

Unit 2: Growing plants – Unit 2 Review

The objectives for this lesson are that students should be able to:

- Check what they have learned about growing plants in this unit

- Find out how they are working towards, within and beyond the Grade 1 level.

Note: *items in italic are this Unit's scientific enquiry expectations.*

At the end of this Unit Students working towards Grade 1 level will:

- name some common plants

- identify leaf, root, stem and flower

- recognize that plants need water to grow

- recognize that plants are found in some outside places

- *make simple comparisons.*

In addition students working within Grade 1 level will:

- recognize that plants are living

- recognize that plants need water and light to grow

- recognize that different plants are found in different places

- *explore the conditions plants need for growth*

- *record the stages of plant growth*

- *follow instructions.*

Further to this, students working beyond Grade 1 level will:

- describe differences between plants grown in the light and in the dark

- suggest how to find out about what plants need in order to grow well

- *communicate what they found out*

- *make simple predictions.*

This question allows the student to demonstrate that they have a clear understanding that plants and animals are alive. Use their list to then judge whether things like the table or chair or a tree, etc. are alive or not.

Use the Unit 2 assessment to check the students' understanding of the content of the unit. The answers are given below.

Name: _____ Date: _____

WS 10 Unit 2 Assessment

1 Write the correct label on each line:

Makes food
Makes seeds
Holds up the plant

2 Tick (✓) the words for a plant that is short of water.

| healthy | yellow | limp | straggly | wilted | green |

3 Tick (✓) the words for a plant that is short of light.

| healthy | yellow | limp | straggly | wilted | green |

4 Anna found a pot plant. It was in a dark, dry corner. She wanted to help it grow. What should she do?

_____

_____

_____

10   Heinemann Explore Science Grade 1

Written assessment

Answers to Workbook WS 10, Unit 2 review

1 Flower – makes seeds
   Leaf   – makes food
   Stem   – holds up the plant

2 wilted, limp ticked

3 yellow, straggly ticked

4 She should put it in the light and water it regularly.

The answer!

Why do we call some plants weeds? (See page 11, *Student Book*)

A weed is a plant growing in the wrong place. Use the 'alive' criteria to ensure the students know a weed is alive. Then look at its parts and discuss if it could be a plant or an animal. At this stage they only have these two groups to choose from!

And finally...

According to the traditional fairy tale of *Jack and the Beanstalk*, magic beans grew into a towering beanstalk that reached through the clouds overnight. Although the students' bean plants will take a little longer to grow, growing plants at any stage makes an interesting display. Make a class beanstalk using paper leaves and trail it around your classroom; add leaves to it as the students' plants grow.

Create a table display of plants we use. Think about unusual plants and their uses, such as coffee beans, vanilla pods, tea leaves, papyrus, paper and rubber.

Unit 3: Sorting and using materials

The objectives for this Unit are that students should be able to:

- Use their senses to explore and describe common materials

- Know the characteristics of many types of materials

- Sort objects into groups based on the properties of their materials

- Make predictions and carry out investigations to test their ideas

- Record their findings using pictures, words and tables.

SB pp.21–32   *Science background*

We live in a material word – in more ways than one! Everything around us is a material. Students' early experiences of materials lay the foundation for future science work in chemistry. Use the lesson ideas to give plenty of opportunities for students to explore, use and change a wide range of everyday materials.

Variety of 'materials'

In everyday language, the word 'material' is generally used for fabrics. Students need to know that in science all the 'stuff' around us is made of different materials. Materials come in all shapes and sizes, with different properties, and they are used for different purposes. Materials include not only solids but also liquids and gases. Even food and water are materials. Much classroom work uses sheet materials (such as paper, plastic, etc.), so be sure to include other materials in your discussions such as rocks, powders, plants and liquids. It is tempting to think of materials as the things used to make other products: wood, stone, plastic, etc. This Unit also explores food and drink (as does Unit 1) as examples of materials.

Students often confuse the name of an object with the material it is made of (e.g. 'window' is not a material but 'glass' is). Use examples of materials rather than actual objects as far as possible, particularly when introducing names and properties (e.g. a piece of metal rather than a shaped spoon).

Students may not know the name of a material. Some materials are made to look like others (such as wood laminates on furniture or plastics looking like metal on mobile phone fascias).

To broaden students' knowledge of materials ask students what different objects are made of. What are the windows made of? The walls? The chairs? Many objects will be made with more than one material. Chairs may have plastic seats, metal legs and rubber feet. Walls may be made of brick or plasterboard, with paint on the surface and wooden skirting boards.

Properties

The same material can exist in many different forms. Paper is a good, everyday example of material that has many different uses depending on its properties. It can be made absorbent (paper towels) or water-resistant (greaseproof paper); it can be strong (like brown wrapping paper) or weak (like tissue paper). Plastics can be made with very different properties – thin or thick, flexible or rigid, transparent or opaque. For example, clingfilm has very different uses to a car bumper but both are made of plastic.

Paper

Remember the three Rs to help protect the environment: reduce; re-use; recycle. Paper is made from trees. Nearly one third of the Earth's land surface is covered in trees and, as long as new planting replaces the trees we use, this raw material should not run out. Recycling paper can save trees as well as saving manufacturing energy. The fibres in paper get broken up into shorter and shorter strands each time it is recycled. So although many newspapers now have a significant recycled component, the quality deteriorates until the fibres are only useful for rough cardboard packaging material. Paper is made by separating the fibres in wood (pulp) and joining them again in a criss-cross pattern to make thin sheets of paper. If you tear a sheet of paper you will see the tiny fibres stuck together at the edge (use a magnifying glass). Different types of paper and cardboard are made depending on the quality of the wood used, the chemicals added to it, and the dyes to colour it.

Glass

Glass is made with molten sand. It is one of the oldest artificial materials, first made around 5000 years ago. It is transparent, easily moulded into different shapes, hard, and slow to decay. This is why glass has so many uses in our lives as bottles, glasses, windows, spectacles, and more.

Changing materials' properties

Scientists distinguish different types of materials, and use the fact that they have distinct properties to use them for different jobs. Scientists can also change and improve a material's properties as well as make new materials.

Many materials are treated in some way to improve their properties. Fabrics may be waterproofed by adding silicone resin, which repels water. This makes coats, tents and umbrellas water-resistant. We can also waterproof materials by coating them with wax or oils. Substances derived from oil share some of the properties of plastics in repelling water. Materials can be reinforced to make them stronger. Glass and plastics may be reinforced with wire. Some materials can be polished to make their surfaces shinier and more attractive. Metals are strong, long lasting, and only melt at very high temperatures. They are also good conductors of electricity and heat.

Magnetism

Many metals are alloys (made from more than one metal). Adding small amounts of other materials to iron makes steel, increasing its flexibility. Ferrous metals (those which contain iron) are magnetic. Steel 'tin' cans (made of steel thinly coated in tin to prevent corrosion) are magnetic, but aluminium ones are not, so magnets are used to separate the two types of can for recycling. The recycling logos on cans often show whether they are made of steel or aluminium. Iron-based metals can be magnetized by stroking them with a magnet – that is why some pins or paper clips can stick to each other – but this magnetism is only temporary.

Language

***Absorbent** It soaks up liquids.

Fabric A textile or cloth.

***Ferrous metal** A metal containing iron.

Gas A material that has weight but no shape.

Liquid A material that flows and has a flat top.

Magnetic Attracted to a magnet.

Material All the 'stuff' around us – solid, liquid or gas.

Properties The qualities of materials.

Solid A material that holds its shape.

***State** The condition of a material: solid, liquid or gas.

Waterproof A material which does not let water through.

* Technical definitions generally for teachers, not students, at this stage.

Key vocabulary

The following words might be introduced or used with the children alongside others, to accustom them to the nature of scientific vocabulary:

communicate	predict
describe	record
feel	sort/group
observe	test

These words may be of use in terms of comparisons:

attract	plastic
bendy/flexible	repel
cold	rough
colour	shape
dry	smell
foods	smooth
hand	soft
heavy	stiff/rigid
light (weight)	texture
magnetic	warm
materials	wet
metal	wood

Resources

A full list of resources is located at the end of the introduction to the *Teacher's Book* for ease of gathering resources. Many resources will already be in the classroom, but a few may need prior arrangement. For example:

- Different types of paper (towels, kitchen paper, writing paper).

59

- A selection of magnets.

- Magnetic and non-magnetic materials, including steel and aluminium cans.

- Drinking straws, jars and droppers.

- A selection of sheet materials, including plastics as well as woven fabrics.

- Waterproofing substances such as wax, oil, petroleum jelly.

- The reader *Sorting and Using Materials* may be used with this Unit.

Visit a local museum or use a collection of historical objects to find out about materials. Include less obvious examples such as fur or feathers, as well as common examples such as flour or sugar. All materials are physical things taking up space (even liquids and gases). Talk about the materials used to make clothes, but reinforce the point that materials are not just fabrics. Your own body is made up of materials. Students may not think of their skin or bone as a material. *What are animal skins or fish bones used for?*

Scientists are always trying to create new materials. Materials have had to be designed which are very light, as well as able to resist extreme temperatures and forces, to go into outer space. *Why do astronauts have very heavy boots when they land on the Moon?*

Talk about special materials such as reflective clothing that shows up in the dark or wet-suits that keep you warm in the sea.

Bright ideas

How are materials made stronger?

- The webs, bends and folds in many domestic objects add strength to weak sheet materials. If you use scissors to cut the rim off a plastic or paper disposable cup, it loses its rigidity. Look at a lunch box, or an ice cream container: the rim, folds and corner 'webs' all add strength to the structure. The folded edges of boxes and baking trays add strength to sheets that would otherwise bend under the load. Try some simple paper sculpture. The shapes add strength to the material.

- Test tubes of different kinds, where the shape adds strength. Rolling a sheet of paper makes a pillar that can support a pile of books. Standing a board on four card tubes makes a 'stool' that will carry a (safely supported) student.

How are materials made weaker?

- Look for examples from the perforations on a kitchen roll to the creasing of the joins on sweet wrappers.

How are two or more materials combined to make the best of both?

- Strong blockboard is covered with an attractive veneer; plastic can be metalized to look like steel or copper. Find and research examples of some or all of these, and record 'amazing materials' for others.

Knowledge check

Students should know about the five senses and related vocabulary (see Unit 1 *Ourselves and other animals*).

Skills check

Students need to:
- be able to name and describe common materials (or at least objects made from them).

- know that there are many types of materials (not just fabrics) with different characteristics.

- be able to group materials on this basis.

- learn how the characteristics of materials make them suitable for particular uses.

- learn how we can change them to make them more useful for us.

Some students will:
- use observation and communication skills

- learn to predict as well as turn ideas into a form that can be tested

- record their findings with simple pictures, words and tables.

Encourage students to use all their senses when describing materials and to use as many words as they can think of that would apply to a particular material.

Links to other subjects

Literacy: Distinguishing everyday language from scientific language. Naming materials. Developing descriptive words for the properties of materials. The use of opposites and of similes. Writing labels, annotating diagrams. Creative writing. Poetry and drama. Following simple instructions. Reading fiction (stories and rhymes). Using information books. Recording data in charts and tables. Talking about what they are doing and what they find out. Taking part in group discussions.

Numeracy: Sorting materials into groups and matching. Using a Venn diagram for overlapping groups. Describing shapes, using 3D shapes. Counting.

Art/Design technology: Work on materials has strong links to design and make activities in design technology, and to art and design. It can link to ICT with the use of the Internet and CD-ROMs.

Let's find out...

This Unit opens with this question:

Could you drink hot tea from a tea cup made of chocolate?

A chocolate 'anything' is always a motivating starter! You could model chocolate spoons in hot milk to show what happens in a warm place.

Unit 3: Sorting and using materials – What's it like?

The objectives for this lesson are that students should be able to:

- Understand that the word 'material' covers many objects, not just fabric

- Use their senses to explore materials

- Describe the properties of materials, including how they look and feel

- Compare materials, looking at similarities and differences.

SB p.22

Starter

- What materials can the class see around them? Make a list on a large sheet of paper. Invite students to add to the list when they think of more examples. Distinguish the material an object is made of from its name. Students may not know the actual material, particularly as some materials are made to look like others. Let them question you. Prompt more words for the materials list. *What is the bookshelf made of? What about the cabinet in the corner?* Many objects will be made with more than one material, so keep prompting them.

- Looking round the classroom can elicit a range of materials. Some are harder to spot than others as they are highly coloured or variations of plastic or they are plastic coated metal. Try to start off with a range of objects that are made of clearly recognizable material, for example wooden spoons, metal cutlery, plastic trays, etc.

Explain

Students may describe objects rather than the materials themselves. Allow this to happen. Then move them on to describe the material once they are more confident with the topic.

Which one?

Recap the senses from previous work and discuss which one might be best to explore materials. *Which one does a baby use a lot?* (Taste.) *Is that wise? Why not?*

Provide each student with the same material and ask each to try to come up with a word to describe how it feels. Have a class vote for the best one. Do this for a range of materials. Challenge the students to use words starting with different letters of the alphabet, so that a wider range of vocabulary is developed.

Things to do

- Either blindfold students or use a feely box (or bag) to hide different objects in turn. One student puts their hand in and uses words to describe the object. The rest of the class have to guess what it might be. Include some challenging materials such as fake fur, cork tiles, etc.

- Once they have grasped describing the object, move onto describing the material it is made from.

- In small groups, take it in turns to describe different materials using each different sense. What does it look like, feel like, sound like, smell like and (if safe) taste like?

- Develop language by matching opposite meanings and developing similes.

Differentiation

Encourage more able students to use more scientific words for their descriptions or to use one sense at a time to describe the material.

Did you know?

'Material' is commonly used to describe fabric.

Dig deeper

Introduce a glass of water or a cold drink. Ask students what materials they can see. They will probably say the glass, metal can or plastic bottle. If they don't mention it, ask: *Is water a material? What other materials are there? So are there any ones safe to eat?*

I wonder...

Possibly the rarest material that the students will be aware of is gold or platinum. This is partly why it commands a high price.

Other ideas

WS 11

- Develop the concept of opposites: hard and soft, shiny and dull, rough and smooth, solid and liquid. What other pairs can students think of? Extend students' descriptive language by introducing new words when appropriate, such as rigid or transparent.

- Develop their language with common sayings like 'as hard as nails', 'as dry as a bone', 'as cold as ice'. Can students make up their own similes?

- Play a game of materials 'Snap!', or use WS 11 to match objects to materials.

Presentation

Start to produce a display of adjectives to describe materials and images to go with them.

Plenary

- Ask students to describe a material with as many different words as they can. Write a list. *Which material has the most words linked to it?* Play a quick-fire quiz game naming opposites. *What is the opposite of hard, thick, light, rough, etc ...?*

- Design a new material for the future: *What would it look and feel like? What uses would it have?*

Unit 3: Sorting and using materials – A lot of materials

The objectives for this lesson are that students should be able to:

- Use communication skills to identify and describe materials

- Group materials by type and by properties

- Understand that different objects can be made from the same material

- Make a labelled wall display containing materials.

SB p.23

Starter

- Put a range of materials on display, for example aluminium foil, a metal bar, a mirror, clingfilm, Plasticine, bone, feathers, shells, and safe powders such as sugar or flour. Encourage students to handle and describe the materials.

Explain

The difference between artificial and natural materials is unclear. Some materials are made from natural produce, like paper and cardboard which come from wood. Technically any material that has been altered by people is artificial, so paper is artificial, but a wooden spoon wouldn't be, as the original material is still recognizable and has only been shaped, not changed. Students may find this hard to grasp.

⚠️ Make sure any materials that students handle have no sharp edges or other risks. Avoid using glass.

Things to do

- Use a collection of materials for students to group. Suggest some categories to start – which materials are hard or soft, rough or smooth? Can they group all plastics, woods or metals together? Look at the variety of ways that they can be grouped, including colour. Is colour a criterion? Colours can be changed.

- Look closely at two examples of the same material that appear very different, such as rigid coloured plastic and clear clingfilm (or aluminium foil and a metal bar). Ask students to describe as many similarities and differences as they can. Ensure the students understand that both are examples of the same sort of material.

Differentiation

More able students can pair up materials that have opposite properties such as bendy or rigid. Ask them to find out what was used for everyday objects before plastics – spoons, bags, bowls, and brushes, for example.

Did you know?

Sand is heated up to very high temperatures and a chemical change takes place producing glass.

Dig deeper

Many plastics are made from oil.

I wonder…

Some precious gemstones may well be the students' initial answer, or even gold. However, the most expensive material in the world is also the one that is the rarest – by definition. In general terms, the most expensive thing that the students will possibly have come across will be emeralds, as this is the most expensive gemstone, and platinum as the most expensive 'precious' metal. Ask the students why they think it is the most expensive metal.

Other ideas

WS 12

- In small groups, make shoebox scenes of different rooms of a doll's house using actual materials such as fabric for curtains, carpet on the floor, wood for chairs.

- Cover small 'treasure' boxes with different materials such as shells, felt, foil. *Who might own the box? What might they keep in it?*

- Have a number of types of materials along with objects made from them. For example, aluminium foil and an aluminium drinks can, sheep's wool and a woollen jumper, a wooden stick and a wooden spoon (or paper to extend more able students). Ask students to match the material to the object. Can they explain their decisions?

- Use WS 12 to reinforce learning.

- Students can create a simple collage where the actual material is used to represent the image, for example bark or a twig for the trunk of a tree, leaves on the branches, sand as the earth, feathers for a bird.

Presentation

Make a wall display of all the materials students have listed using samples, photographs or drawings. Write the name of each material clearly and add one key property.

Plenary

- Call out the names of objects and see how quickly students can name the material they are made from.

- Use pictures from a shopping catalogue for students to label; include objects made of more than one material such as a metal saucepan with a wooden handle.

65

Unit 3: Sorting and using materials – Common materials

The objectives for this lesson are that students should be able to:

- Take part in a material trail and collect their findings

- Record what they found using words and images

- Communicate their findings, using descriptive vocabulary

- Sort materials into the correct groups.

SB pp.24–25 Starter

- Provide a range of materials for the students to explore and recap their descriptive vocabulary. Ensure that they can name them all.

- Share some images of the groupings made by students in the previous session and ask for the possible names of these groups. If you don't have images, put things into groups yourself or ask a student to help and ask the rest to guess the names of the groups.

The challenge

Ensure that the students use the word 'material' correctly. In common speech, material is often just used to mean cloth or fabric. In science, material is a general word for any substance.

Read the conversation on page 24 of the *Student Book*. Discuss why Rohan would say: 'But the desk isn't made of fabric like our uniforms.' He obviously has a misconception about what materials are.

What to do

Take groups of students on a materials trail around the school – inside and in the grounds. *How many materials can you spot?* Get them to write in the object, and tick what type of material it is. Count them up at the end.

You could take a digital photo to record each material, or do a drawing or take a rubbing.

What you need

- A clipboard and the table and a pencil.

- Possibly a wax crayon or a digital camera for other methods of recording.

What to check

Ensure that the students are able to correctly identify the material of the object, rather than the object itself.

Differentiation

Less able students could use thin paper and a wax crayon held sideways to make rubbings of some textured materials. Help students to name the materials, and label the rubbings.

What did you find?

Which type of material was the most common? How can you tell? Why do you think this is?

Not only can you establish what the most common material is generally, but you may find that the majority of inside materials are man-made, but there are more natural materials outside. *Why?*

Record

Draw a table on the board and discuss what the headings should be with the students. Start with just two columns and ask whether any more are needed.

Encourage the students to record their materials on their table.

Did you know?

You can make a form of plastic in the classroom. Warm a glass of full cream 'whole' milk. Add 4 tablespoons of vinegar. Stir it until lumps begin to form, then strain it and leave the lumps to dry.

Before it sets completely, students can make it into shapes that set.

Plenary

WS 13

- Discuss why there might be fewer objects made from wood or wool. Look around the classroom. *What do you notice about the colours?*

- Show a classroom scene from 100 years ago and one from now. *What differences can be seen in the pictures?*

- Play the game on WS 13. This is a fun way to check understanding of the difference between identifying materials and identifying objects.

Unit 3: Sorting and using materials – The properties of materials

The objectives for this lesson are that students should be able to:

- Learn about some of the properties of materials

- Test materials to see what properties they have

- Find out that all magnetic materials are made of metal

- List the key properties of some materials.

SB p.26

Starter

- Bring in some Brio train track to play with. Discuss what makes the magnetic carriages 'stick' together.

- Give small groups of students magnets to test materials you provide. Test a range of materials to see which are magnetic (include some non-magnetic metals). Put all the magnetic objects in one group and all the non-magnetic ones in another. *What do the magnetic objects have in common? What materials are they made from?* Use the non-magnetic metals to establish that although all the magnetic objects are all metals, not all metals are magnetic.

Explain

Some materials may seem magnetic that are not, for example plastic-coated metal legs on chairs or tables.

> ⚠ Magnets should not be used to test electrical devices. Make sure any empty cans have no sharp edges and are clean.

Drop materials on a protected surface away from feet and be careful when stretching and bending materials. When testing stretch, plan for what will happen if the material breaks.

Things to do

- This is best set up as a circus of activities with stations for testing for magnetism and stations for testing bounce and floatabilty. You could test for stretch or strength too.

- Give small groups of students magnets to test materials.

- Use bowls of water for students to test if materials float or sink. Make sure all the materials are the same or similar shapes as shape affects this test.

- Have a hard surface for dropping materials onto.

- Strength or stretchiness can be tested by attaching part of the material to the wall or a board and pulling against it.

- Use small watering cans to test if something is waterproof or not.

The results should be recorded in a table of ticks and crosses, as each station should have the same materials at it.

Differentiation

More able students can explore a range of unusual materials such a potty putty, or homemade slime (made by adding water slowly to cornflour, stirring all the time, and coloured with food colouring for better effect). They can also collect objects that have unusual properties such as a bendy pencil, shaving foam or a natural sponge.

Did you know?

You will need to tell students at some point in their investigations that only iron and steel (made from iron) are magnetic, as they cannot discover this by first-hand experience. (Some rare metals are magnetic too – but students are unlikely to come across them.)

Dig deeper

Boats are made of metal but they need to be shaped into a hollow so that they float. Plasticine and foil make good modelling materials for this, so you can test this out.

I wonder...

Elastic bands are stretchy. The students could consider what test they could do to test out this question, for example pulling it back (care with snapping) and measuring how far before it snaps, or hanging weight on it until it snaps.

Other ideas

- Play a range of magnet games such as fishing (hang a magnet from a fishing rod and pick up paper fish with paper clip 'noses'), magnetic marbles, etc.

- *What would life be like if clothing wasn't stretchy?* Examine some woollen socks and modern socks with elastic in them. *What would it be like if your socks didn't have elastic in them?*

- Make up a game such as magnetic racing cars where the magnet is hidden under the table. The cars have a paperclip on them.

Presentation

Place the materials into sorting hoops to show their properties.

Take each material in turn and list its key properties, for example metals are usually cold to touch, shiny, hard and strong and resist corrosion, so are long lasting. Plastics are usually warm to touch, smooth, sometimes transparent, and can be moulded into shape. 'Warm materials' reflect back your body heat. 'Cold materials' conduct it away from you.

Plenary

- Discuss some situations where: a magnet might save the day, such as recovering a key dropped down the drain, or where being strong could save you, like having a strong seatbelt, or being stretchy and keeping your socks up.

- Ask students to decide which is the 'best' material in the group tested. *Why? Is it the one that has the most properties or just one you like?*

69

Unit 3: Sorting and using materials – What's its job?

The objectives for this lesson are that students should be able to:

- Understand that materials are matched to the job they do by their properties

- Find out that the same object can be made from different materials

- Discover that some materials do not work well in some jobs

- Record and explain what they have found out.

SB p.27 — *Starter*

- Remind students of the tests they carried out in a previous session and what properties certain materials might need.

Explain

Students may not be aware that some materials are used for a job because they are cheaper or more easily available than others.

Best for the job

'Best' is not a scientific word. It does not describe a quality or property. A material may be the 'best' conductor, for example, but it will not be the 'best' insulator.

Start a group brainstorm to suggest inappropriate uses of materials, such as a chocolate saucepan or metal shoes. *Why wouldn't they work?*

Students make up and complete sentences in the form. 'Glass is used for windows because ....'

Which spoon?

Collect examples of the same type of object made from different materials such as plastic, wooden and metal spoons or forks. *Which is best for which task? Why? What do you mean by 'best'?*

Things to do

- Use *Student Book* page 27 to discuss why different objects are made from different materials. *What other materials could you substitute to do the same job?*

- Provide a range of common materials, and ask the students to sort them by properties.

- Make a collection of boxes made of different materials (wood, plastic, metal, cardboard). Students can list what they would use each for. *Why is plastic better for storing food?*

How many materials are in a car or a house?

If you can, take the class outside to look at a real car. Or use the image on page 27 of a house contents. Ask questions about what things are made of and why they are, linking back to the properties from a previous session.

For example, for the car: what the seats are made of, the tyres, the dashboard, etc. Talk about why the body is made of metal, the windows are made of toughened glass, the tyres made of rubber and the bumpers made of plastic.

For example, for the house: what the doors of a house are made of, the windows, the roof, the curtains, etc.

> ⚠ If viewing a real car, take care about where it is parked and other cars in the vicinity.

Differentiation

More able students can brainstorm a material and all the things made from it, such as: rubber tyres, bands, boots; glass windows, spectacles, bottles, mirrors, etc. Introduce materials with specialist uses such as reflective or thermal materials. Use catalogue pictures to stick object pictures in groups by material.

Did you know?

Many original cars and even aeroplanes had a wooden frame with canvas stretched over the top and then painted with a resin to make them hard.

However, these weren't very strong or safe if there was an accident.

Dig deeper

Scientists are always inventing new materials. There some called 'smart materials' which behave counter intuitively, for example one that is stretched and gets fatter rather than thinner. Some of these make their way into everyday use, for example Teflon for baking on, which was developed for the space shuttle.

I wonder...

Concrete shoes would make walking impossible.

Other ideas

* Revise and consolidate teaching about materials and their uses.

* When reading stories, stop and ask students why something is made of a particular material. Whenever something new arises ('the knight put on his armour', 'the guard closed the castle door') ask what it was made from. Why?

Presentation

Use images from stories or the classroom on a wall to label with materials that you wouldn't use.

Substitute a material used in a story for one with a different property. *What would happen in this story now?*

Plenary

* *Why are some houses made of bricks or concrete when in some hot countries they may be made of sticks or straw?*

* Discuss the least suitable materials for a job. *Why is a window pane not made of wood? Why is a pencil not made of glass?*

Unit 3: Sorting and using materials – Don't get wet

The objectives for this lesson are that students should be able to:

- Understand that some materials are, or can be made, waterproof

- Make predictions and observations of different materials when water is poured on them

- Discover how to make materials waterproof and test their examples

- Describe and record their results.

Starter

SB p.28

- Make sure the students know the names and the sequence of the seasons. Make sure they can relate the weather appropriate to each season. Show a range of images of people dressed for different seasons, such as hot, rainy, cold, and so on. Then ask them to match the people to their season. Take each person in turn. *How are they appropriately dressed for that season?* Although water's 'wetness' is one of its most useful properties, we spend a lot of our time protecting ourselves from it.

- Talk about the things we might use to keep us dry in the rain, for example umbrellas and wellington boots. Houses keep the rain out; boats keep the people and cargo inside dry.

Explain

Students may not be familiar with waterproofing substances such as wax. Point out they are often greasy substances.

I'm soaked

This may be a new word. Introduce the idea of waterproof with the starter activities and then introduce the word once they have grasped its meaning. Oracy before literacy!

Which clothes when?

Show some season-appropriate clothes and ask the students to match them to the pictures of the weather. Ask the students what materials have been used to make the clothes – both the real clothes and the ones in the picture. Accept reasonable guesses – most fabrics are made from mixed materials, often combining natural and man-made, to utilize the best qualities of each. Drip water on to different materials, a few drops at a time. Students predict, then observe and describe what happens.

> ⚠ Be aware of the suffocation dangers of plastics with younger students.

Things to do

Make mini umbrellas

Develop students' practical skills. The students' investigation requires careful manipulation skills to make the umbrellas and to use a dropper. Practise using the dropper first.

Make some mini umbrellas. Use half a length of a plastic drinking straw with one end split into four to make the spokes of the umbrella. Cut circles of different materials to fit on to the umbrella. Try paper, cloth, plastic, etc. Slowly drip water onto the top of the umbrella until it leaks. *How many drops can each material take?*

Record

Students can record the results as a bar chart with a dot or round sticker for each water drop the umbrella held back. Start to develop this skill further. (To see when the umbrella leaks use water coloured with food colouring and possibly put a sugar cube directly underneath.)

Discuss which materials worked well.

Differentiation

More able students can discuss and group materials into those that are waterproof (such as plastic), and those that can be made waterproof by treating them in some way (such as fabric). Putting the water in jars, sealed with different materials and then inverting them over the sink produces exciting results. Count until the water comes through.

Did you know?

Challenge the students to see if they can improve the performance of some materials by waterproofing. *What could you use?* For example, wax crayons, shoe polish, cooking oil, furniture polish or petroleum jelly.

Compare their waterproofing properties by rubbing them all over the pieces of material. Now count how many drops of water the umbrella will take. Students then plot the drops on the same chart using a different coloured dot or sticker to highlight the effectiveness of the waterproofing.

Dig deeper

An oilskin is a fisherman's set of outer waterproof garments are coated in a layer of oil to ensure they are waterproof. Oil floats on water and the two don't mix. Wax does this too.

I wonder....

Metal is 'waterproof' but it isn't a good material to make into an umbrella or clothing. Ask the students for their ideas on this.

Other ideas

- Brainstorm all the things the class can think of that need to be waterproof. Ask questions to prompt students' thinking. Examples may include rubber gloves, painting aprons, shower caps or curtains, fish bowls, baths and sinks. *What materials are these made of? Do they need to keep the water in or keep the water out? What would happen if they were not waterproof?*

- Use information books or the Internet to find out about monsoons. Talk about the effects the weather has on what we can or can't do in our everyday lives.

Presentation

Display the results of the waterproofing activity along with a series of waterproof items such as an umbrella, sou'wester, pair of wellington boots, wax jacket, etc.

Plenary

- Use the activity to review the previous work in this Unit on the properties of materials. *Would you make a pair of shoes out of paper? Why not? Would you make an umbrella out of wool? Why not?*

- Can students discuss different degrees of waterproofing – showerproof, stormproof?

Unit 3: Sorting and using materials – Paper

The objectives for this lesson are that students should be able to:

- Recognize that materials such as paper can be used in different ways

- Learn what purposes paper is good for

- Compare the properties of different types of paper

- Test different papers and record their results.

SB p.29 ## Starter

- Make a collection of all the different types of paper found around the school and home. Include tissues, kitchen towel, toilet paper, tracing paper, wrapping paper, newspaper, writing paper, greeting cards, etc.

- Discuss the name and use of each type of paper. *How are these papers different? Can you describe how they are alike, too?*

Explain

Explain that almost all papers are made from the same raw material, wood.

An adult can use a food processor to break up the fibres in the recycling paper activity more quickly.

Things to do

Testing different papers

Challenge students to test different papers. Which would be the best to write on; wrap a parcel with; make paper aeroplanes with; soak up a spill, etc.? Explore:

- How will students keep their tests fair?

- Can they predict the outcomes?

- How can they record their results?

- Can they give each paper a star rating?

Grouping different papers

Ask students to group papers depending on their properties.

- Which are strong?

- Which are absorbent?

- Which let light through (are translucent)?

Use a Venn diagram to include papers that have more than one property.

Use a magnifying glass to look at the fibres in paper more closely. Research and discuss how paper is made from wood.

Recycling papers

Students can recycle their own paper.

- Tear newspaper into small pieces. Soak these in warm water for several days until they become pulp.

- Dip a fine mesh (such as a flat sieve) into the pulp and spread some pulp evenly across it.

- Put an absorbent cloth on top and press down gently to squeeze out as much water as possible.

- Carefully sandwich the pulp between newspapers, and weigh it down. The paper will dry naturally but you could iron it flat or cut it into shape.

- Add flower petals, sequins, coloured threads to the pulp to make decorative papers or greeting cards.

Students could recycle different types of waste paper (kitchen or tissue paper). Test which is the strongest or looks best.

Differentiation

More able students can look at two types of the same paper, such as different quality kitchen towels, and describe their similarities and differences. Look at how some papers are changed to improve their properties (such as the 'pockets' supposed to increase the absorbency of a kitchen towel). Test their effectiveness.

Did you know?

Rice paper is made from rice and as such can be eaten. Very thin pieces of rice paper are made for cake decorating – the ones with your own picture on that you can purchase from some cake shops and supermarkets for birthdays.

Dig deeper

It takes 24 trees to make a tonne of newspaper. If we recycle paper, we save 17 trees.

I wonder....

The first paper was made in China about two thousand years ago.

Other ideas

- Look at examples of recycled paper – writing pads, kitchen towels, etc. *Do they look any different from other paper?* Find out from information books, the Internet or a visit to a recycling plant what happens in the recycling process. Create a paper recycling scheme in school if one does not exist.

- Look at specialist papers such as rice paper, wax paper and blotting paper. *How do the properties of the paper match its use?*

- Make paper stronger by folding it. *How many times can you fold the same sized piece of different types of paper?*

- Collect cardboard of different strengths (from boxes, different types of tubes, etc.). Try bending each to see which is strongest. Look at how cardboard is strengthened with folds and creases, or by making it corrugated.

- Find ways of joining paper together, temporarily with folds or paperclips, or permanently with staples or glue.

Presentation

Make posters for different types of paper advertising why they are best for particular purposes.

Challenge students to make the strongest shape they can with a sheet of A4 paper. Fold it, roll it, and corrugate it. *Can sheets of paper support the weight of a housebrick?* (Yes, if they roll four paper columns for it to stand on.) Display these for all to see and judge.

Plenary

- Collect paper and cardboard used in packaging. Include sweet papers and crisp packets (plastic as well as paper), envelopes and boxes. Talk about why each does a good job. How can they distinguish between the paper and plastic packaging?

- *What paper would you use to draw a picture, wrap a present, and carry vegetables? Why?* Ask students why it is important to recycle paper. *How can you use less paper?*

New International Edition

Unit 3: Sorting and using materials – All bagged up

The objectives for this lesson are that students should be able to:

- Find out if different materials can do the same job

- Plan and carry out a scientific investigation to test bags

- Record their results in a chart

- Consider whether they found the best material for the job.

SB pp.30–31 Starter

- Talk about materials that are used for different purposes, and why.

- Introduce the same object made from different materials such as plastic, paper and fabric bags. *When would you use each type and why? Which bag would be best to carry a wet swimming towel?* Students can test their bags with wet towels.

The challenge

Share the text and ideas on page 31 of the *Student Book*. Illustrate this with a range of shopping and some bags. You could have some that have already split to illustrate the problem that Benazir and Jamila have.

Carry out a fair test to see if paper, plastic or fabric bags are strongest. At this stage students don't need to be able to plan a fair test but should have some general idea of keeping some things the same to make it 'fair'.

Why do supermarkets use plastic bags if fabric bags are stronger? Discuss recycling and cost if students don't raise them as issues.
Why have some supermarkets introduced a reusable bag?

What to do

Encourage the students to consider the strength of the bags. Some may link strength and size to get all the shopping in.

Hang the bags from the back of a stable chair and carefully add weights to them to see how much they hold. You may need a lot for some bags.

What you need

- Range of supermarket bags, and other bags used for shopping.

- Root vegetables or other large, safe items.

What to check

Ensure that the students add the vegetables/items carefully one at a time and check to see if the bag has changed at all.

> ⚠ Ensure the chair is stable – possibly getting a student to sit on it throughout. Put a cardboard box full of crushed newspaper under the bag to take any fallen items, and to prevent students getting hurt.

Differentiation

Challenge students to wrap a parcel to go through the post (remind them of the work they did on paper in a previous session). They can wrap three identical parcels in paper, plastic and fabric.

Ask another group to act as postal workers, and to test each of the three parcels. They should report back to the wrapping group. Make sure both groups are clear about what they want the packaging to achieve. What are their motives for 'good packaging'?

What did you find?

Benazir and Jamila found that the more expensive hessian bag was best for carrying the shopping.

Record

- Use a prepared table, possibly on the board for students to complete as a class. Each group could test just one bag and then the results collated at the end.

- Take photographs of the bags at the start, and at the end of the test, with the contents piled beside them, and use this as a display.

- Students should record the results as a bar chart with a dot or round sticker for mass that the bag held.

Did you know?

Part of the reason supermarkets have tried to reduce the use of plastic bags, although they are cheap, is that they take so long to rot they are not environmentally friendly.

Many new bags incorporate materials like starch, to rot naturally.

Plenary

Each student can act out a material for the class to identify. They should show with their movements and facial expressions if they are rigid or bendy, hard or soft. Encourage them to mime some things the material may be used for. They can only answer yes or no to questions the class ask as they try to guess the right answer. This will reinforce properties of materials.

Produce a range of spoons of different materials and ask which is best for which job – with cake mixing, eating and cooking things in front of you. This recaps the same use but with different material.

Produce a range of objects made of wood to recap that the same material has lots of uses.

Unit 3: Sorting and using materials – Unit 3 Review

The objectives for this lesson are that students should be able to:

- Check what they have learned about sorting and using materials in this Unit

- Find out how they are working towards, within and beyond, the Grade 1 level.

SB p.32

Expectations

Note: *items in italic are this Unit's scientific enquiry expectations.*

At the end of this Unit students working towards Grade 1 level will:

- make observations of common objects

- communicate these observations.

In addition students working within Grade 1 level will:

- name some common materials

- make observations of common materials

- *communicate these using terms, e.g. bendy, rough, hard*

- *suggest how to test an idea*

- *say what the result of the test shows.*

Further to this, students working beyond Grade 1 level will:

- suggest several reasons why a material may or may not be suitable for a particular purpose

- *predict the results of tests they are going to do.*

Check-up

The saucepan made of a mixture of materials should be placed in the centre between two groups, or within the two hoops of the Venn diagram. Discuss with the students why it is made of more than one material.

Assessment

WS 14

Use the Unit 3 assessment to check the students' understanding of the content of the Unit. The answers are given below.

Name: _____ Date: _____

WS 14

Unit 3 Assessment

1 Circle the words that name a material.

wood   cup   plastic   metal   spoon

2 Complete these sentences.

Wood is usually _____

Metal feels quite _____

Wool or fur feels _____

Glass is used for making _____

Paper is made from _____

3 Draw a line to match the material with the object.

wool   door

metal   jumper

wood   tin can

4 Write the names of four or five materials to go in these groups.

Stiff   Bendy

14   Heinemann Explore Science Grade 1

Written assessment
Answers to Workbook WS 14, Unit 3 review

1   The materials are wood, plastic, metal.

2   Accept sensible suggestions: Wood is usually hard; Metal feels quite cold; Wool or fur feels smooth or soft; Glass is used for making windows, drinking glasses and bottles; Paper is made from wood.

3   wool → jumper; metal → tin can; wood → door.

4   Stiff materials could include wood, metal, glass. Bendy materials include string, Plasticine, rubber bands.

Try to make sure students include the names of some materials if they use names of objects.

The answer!

Could you drink hot tea from a tea cup made of chocolate? (see page 21, Student Book.)

No, you couldn't. A cup made of chocolate would melt once it got hot!

And finally...

Display materials and pictures of materials (both professional ones and students' own photographs, drawings and rubbings) along with the name of the material and the words used to describe its properties around the classroom.

Use objects around the room and label them like this: 'The book is made of paper'; 'The window is made of glass'; 'The door is made of wood'.

Take a large picture of a person or a scene and label all the materials students can see.

Use PE hoops for students to sort collections of materials. *When do the hoops need to overlap to make a third grouping?*

Cover boxes with different material and use each box to store that group of materials (a foil covered box would contain all the metals, a sticky-back plastic box would contain all the plastics).

79

Unit 4: Forces

The objectives for this Unit are that students should be able to:

- Understand the movement of familiar things and that there are different types of forces

- Recognize that both pushes and pulls are forces

- Recognize what makes things speed up, slow down or change direction.

SB pp.33–44   *Science background*

The concepts involved with forces are possibly the most abstract that students will have to address at this level in science. Consequently, most of the activities in this Unit are experiential, encouraging students to identify and describe forces and their effects, rather than asking them to explain what is happening.

Forces are pushes or pulls. We cannot see them but we can observe their effects.

Forces do a number of things:

- they make an object start moving and speed up

- they make an object slow down or stop

- they make a moving object change direction

- they act on an object to change its shape.

The strength of a force can be measured in newtons (N) using a force meter, which students will learn later.

Gravity is the predominant force that we experience. Every object that has a mass also possesses gravity, a force of attraction to another object. However, we do not spend all of our time bumping into each other. This is because the bigger the object, the greater its force of attraction will be. The Earth's mass is so enormous compared to anything on Earth that the force of attraction of all other objects is comparatively negligible. For this reason, we recognize from a very young age that if an object is dropped it will fall straight down towards the ground.

Forced to move

The force of gravity pulls towards the centre of the Earth; its strength decreases with distance. So in outer space, where we are very distant from any other large objects, there is no discernible force of gravity acting on us. We would remain still unless a force acted on us. If someone were to give us a push, we would move in the direction of that push and continue to do so until another force was applied to us. The force is applied to us and then ceased but the motion continues. We do not possess the force that made us move; we are moving in response to it. Students can find this idea very hard to grasp. They may believe that once the force has been applied, it is contained within the object and stays with it until it 'runs out'.

Resisting movement

On Earth, the force of gravity influences the motion of an object. The Earth has an atmosphere that will act against the motion of an object. This is a force which called air resistance. If there were no air resistance, an object falling under the influence of gravity would continue to accelerate until it hit the ground. Air resistance acts against gravity and causes the object to slow down. It also acts against objects moving along, such as bicycles. The faster we cycle, the greater the force of air resistance acting against us will be; we can actually feel it pushing harder against us as we cycle faster. The same effect can be experienced in swimming pools as water resistance. Students may find this easier to understand. We can see and feel water more than air.

Friction is another force that we encounter in everyday life. Friction resists the movement of an object. It acts when two touching surfaces move across each other. Every surface, even the smoothest, has irregularities on it. These interlock when two surfaces are in contact.

If we push a toy car it will begin to slow down a soon as we stop pushing it. This is because the force of friction (as well as air resistance) between the wheels and the surface it is on will resist movement and eventually slow the toy car to a halt.

A balancing act

Objects stay still either because there are no forces acting on them, as in outer space, or because the forces acting on them are balanced. This means that all opposing forces acting on an object are equal. For example, when we sit on a chair the force of gravity pulls us towards the floor but the resisting force of the chair pushes us back. When these two forces are balanced we remain seated.

If as a car is moving forwards it will be receiving a pushing force from the engine. Both air resistance and friction act against this pushing force. If the forces involved are balanced, the car continues to move at a constant speed in a constant direction. If we take our foot off the accelerator pedal, the pushing force of the engine will be smaller than the forces of air resistance and friction. The forces will be unbalanced and the car will slow down.

Wind as force

Air has a force because it has mass. We can see this when the wind blows. Wind is a result of pressure differences on Earth. In hot areas, the air warms up and becomes less dense, creating low air pressure in that area. Air in colder areas will be more dense and will move towards the higher pressure air to redress the imbalance. The movement of these bodies of air causes wind force. It makes things move. The stronger the wind, the greater the pushing force. The direction and strength of the wind has a great influence on our weather.

Language

Air resistance The force from by the air that opposes and resists the motion of an object.

Force A push or pull exerted on an object, usually measured in newtons (N).

Friction The force between two surfaces in contact.

Gravity The force of attraction in all bodies in the universe. It attracts them toward each other, and pulls objects down towards the Earth.

*****Newton (N)** The unit of force.

Pictogram A graph, where each picture represents a separate piece of data.

* Technical definitions generally for teachers, not students, at this stage.

Key vocabulary

The following words might be introduced or used with the children alongside others, to accustom them to the nature of scientific vocabulary:

change	predict
communicate	record
describe	reflect (on prediction)
fair test	start
observe	stop

Resources

A full list of resources is located at the start of the *Teacher's Book* for ease of gathering resources. Many resources will already be in the classroom, but a few may need prior arrangement. For example:

- A tricycle or cart.
- A rope.
- A floor turtle, e.g. Roamer.
- A selection of toy cars.
- A selection of powered toys, e.g. clockwork, battery-operated.
- Books or videos involving builders, e.g. *Bob the Builder.*
- Small wooden blocks and toy bricks.
- An anemometer (a device for measuring wind speed).
- Newspaper weather maps.
- A battery driven hand fan.
- The reader *Pushes and Pulls* may be used with this Unit.

Bright ideas

- Have a road safety campaign, based on pushes and pulls. Show how vehicles cannot stop immediately, and that the faster they are going the longer they will take to come to a halt. Demonstrate also that the faster the vehicle is going, the harder it will hit you. Illustrate the way in which vehicles change direction – that it is not possible for them to turn on the spot, as we can.

- Use toys and teddies to test seat belts. Explore the difference between what happens to a toy resting on a toy car or lorry when it comes to a sudden stop, and one that is strapped to the vehicle. Find out more about seat belts and air bags. The air bag changes shape in an accident; it prevents you hitting the windscreen.

- Make a display of vehicles whose shape reduces air resistance – such as jet aeroplanes, racing yachts and so on.

- Make a marble run where the marble takes the longest time to get from the top to the bottom. How do you speed up or slow down the marble?

- Other ideas to investigate are:

  Make things change direction without touching them by blowing.

  Make a syringe system containing water or air to make things move.

  Investigate the best surface for a ball or a toy car to travel on.

  Investigate which ball is the best bouncer. Count the number of bounces!

Knowledge check

Most students should be able to identify what happens to an object if a force is applied to it, even if they are unable to describe and explain it in terms of the force(s) involved. The reinforcement and building of the language of forces will greatly help students to understand the concepts involved in this Unit.

Skills check

Students need to:

- be able to identify the cause and effect of forces.

- explain what they have observed.

Some students will:

- be able to predict the causal relationships of a force applied to an object.

- understand the link between the strength of the force applied and its effect on the object to which it is applied, for example harder pushes make toy cars go further.

Links to other subject areas

Literacy: Zig-zag book and writing frame suggestions will help students to develop sequenced writing in a reporting genre. Forces also provide descriptive language for students explaining movement.

Numeracy: Use non-standard units to measure the distance that a toy car travels. Look more closely at comparative bar charts by using strips of paper, or ribbon, to measure the distance travelled and then turn them into a bar chart for display.

Other subjects: Discussions on road safety and building sites can easily be extended into other areas of personal safety.

Through Drama, students can illustrate forces and their effects. Students can respond to verbal descriptions of ways that things move and interpret them through their actions.

ICT: There are a number of ICT opportunities. As well as using the Roamer to cover elements of control, the Roamer World software also has a number of activities for young students to undertake these tasks on-screen.

Let's find out...

This Unit opens with the question:

Could you get dressed if you could only push, and not pull?

Most of the time when you pull you push too. *Take a look at putting on socks, your foot has to push whilst you pull on the sock!*

New International Edition

Unit 4: Forces – Moving around

The objectives for this lesson are that students should be able to:

- Learn their left and right
- Understand that there are many different types of movement
- Follow simple instructions about how to move
- Use different words to explain movement.

SB p.34

Starter

- Find out what students already know about movement. Let them demonstrate how they can move in different ways, for example directionally (forwards, backwards), sideways (left and right), up, down, spinning. Ask them how they could get other students to move and to demonstrate, for example (gently) pushing/pulling and turning them around.

- Take the students into the playground. Ask students to identify activities involving people moving or being moved.

- Create a word wall of already-familiar movement words. Add to it throughout the Unit.

Explain

Most students will know common directional words but some may have little idea of left and right.

The information helps students understand left and right.

> ⚠ Students will need to show self control and take care when undertaking activities that involve pushing/pulling each other.

Things to do

- In the hall or playground, ask students to spread out, making sure they can hear you. Give them commands such as, *Take one step forwards, Crouch down, Left hand up,* and so on, as part of a 'Simon says' game.

- Once students are familiar with the type of instructions, let them take turns to instruct others.

- Develop the vocabulary of different types of movement.

- Play the 'Hokey Cokey'. Who can put their hands in and out correctly?

- Develop students' ability to give directional instructions by using a floor turtle like Roamer. *How can you move Roamer from one part of the classroom to another?*

Differentiation

Some students have trouble with left and right, especially when given as movement instructions. Use directional arrows (don't just point) instead. Similarly, use picture labels/numbers/letters/colours on walls to direct students. Reduce the cues as the students gain confidence.

Did you know?

Although the majority of people are right handed, take care that left-handed students don't feel 'odd'.

When playing ball games, for example football, some students may use a different foot to the hand they write with.

Dig deeper

Recognizing 'clockwise' as a turn to the right is helpful when planning to give directions, for example quarter turn clockwise, to a digital device, for example a floor turtle or Roamer.

I wonder...

Build up a word bank of other ways in which our bodies can move, for example: roll, bend, twist; and directions, backwards, forwards and so on.

Other ideas

- Pair up similar-sized students. *Who can push/ pull? How can you tell? Which way do you move? Do you move towards each other or away from each other when you push?* For safety reasons, students should do this sitting or kneeling. Reduce the risk of someone getting pulled or pushed over.

- Discuss why we have to be careful when we are moving around. We need to be aware of people and things around us so that we don't bump into them. Discuss safety in school. *Why shouldn't you run in the corridors?* Let students make up their own set of classroom safety rules and display them.

- Develop a 'Follow me' game in small groups in the classroom. Encourage smaller movements using different vocabulary. For example, *can you wiggle your finger/twitch your nose/move only one finger?* Let students take turns in leading the activity.

Presentation

Create a display board of images of the students moving in different ways and words to describe these. If these are pinned to the wall they can be moved about to test movement vocabulary.

Plenary

- A supervised visit to a safe, clean playground will reinforce understanding. Can students explain how they are moving as they play on the apparatus?

- How well are students able to follow instructions? Can they identify possible dangers to themselves and others through their actions or the equipment that they are using? Can they suggest possible changes to make an activity safer?

- Students will most likely have seen footage of people moving in space or on the Moon. *How would it feel to be weightless? What would it be like if our classroom was in outer space?*

Unit 4: Forces – Moving things around

The objectives for this lesson are that students should be able to:

- Suggest how objects can be made to move and check whether their predictions were correct

- Understand the difference between a push and a pull

- Find out that the harder the force, the further the movement

- Communicate their observations.

SB p.35 | Starter

- Struggle to get into the drawer of your desk. Get quite frustrated and talk about how you really need to get in there, but no matter how hard you push, you can't do it. Encourage the students to try. If they tell you or show you to pull, talk about the differences.

- Tell students that 'force' is the scientific word for a push or a pull. You need forces to make things move. What is there in the classroom that can be moved with a push force or a pull force?

Explain

Students may not clearly distinguish between things that they move and things that move under their own power. Emphasize the push supplied by the student in terms of direction of the push and direction that the object moves.

⚠ Take sensible precautions over any moving activities.

Things to do

- Reinforce the use of the word 'force' when describing pushes and pulls.

- Give students a set of sticky notes labelled 'things we push', 'things we pull' and 'things we push and pull'. Stick them together on objects in the classroom. Emphasize 'push force' and 'pull force' as students demonstrate the pushes and pulls that they make on the objects. For example, 'I use a pull force to open the drawer and a push force to close the drawer.'

- Go on a 'things that move' hunt. Photograph things that move with a push force or a pull force. Photograph students pushing and pulling the things that they find, too.

Differentiation

Add the word 'force' to their current vocabulary. For those who find this hard, keep emphasizing 'push force' and 'pull force' as phrases to use.

Did you know?

Generally we use either a push or a pull to make something move, but some objects can be moved both ways, for example a gliding chair, or a toy car. Some things need us to push and to pull at the same time, like pulling on a jumper whilst pushing your arms through the sleeves.

Dig deeper

Gravity is the force that holds us on the Earth.

I wonder...

It is easier to pull down than to pull or push up. A rope over a branch makes it easier to lift a heavy object.

Other ideas

- Sort classroom toys into items that can be pushed/pulled or both. Make sure that there are plenty of toys for each group and that no electrical or battery-operated toys are included. Emphasize that it is the push/pull force that makes the toy move.

- Develop this by providing some toys that move by themselves, for example clockwork toys, battery-operated toys, pull back and let go cars, etc. Encourage students to describe their movement and recognize what provides force that makes the toy move.

- When students get dressed after PE, provide instructions about putting their clothes on – get some wrong and question students about whether you can 'push' your socks on etc.

Presentation

Create a collage of items from a magazine that need to be pushed to move them, including clothes and cutlery.

Let students create a 'push/pull diary' for a short time to record daily what they have pushed and/or pulled. Restrict it to five items to keep it manageable.

Plenary

- Display items that can be moved by pushing, by pulling, and by doing both. Create a type of Venn diagram with interconnecting sets. Let students create their own diagram by drawing objects in sets. They can use ideas from the display as well as add their own. Very heavy items that students could not move by either pushing or pulling should be drawn outside the sets.

- Identify the obvious visible effects of forces in the immediate environment. A 'forces spotting walk' through school provides an opportunity to recognize that all movement is related to a force being applied.

New International Edition

Unit 4: Forces – Using pushes and pulls

The objectives for this lesson are that students should be able to:

- Explore pushes and pulls in their lives
- Make predictions about what they might find out in their investigations
- Collect evidence so they can answer questions
- Record their results in a graph.

SB pp.36–37

Starter

- Read or watch some *Bob the Builder* stories, asking students to point out movement and push/pull forces in the stories.
- Discuss the machines that help *Bob the Builder* to do his work. What sort of movements does each of them make? How do their names (Rolley, Lofty, Dizzy, etc.) relate to the way they move or the jobs they do? Can you think of any other good names for machines used on a building site? Let students draw their own machines and make Plasticine/junk models of them.
- Introduce all the things found in a playground to play on. *How do you make them move?*

The challenge

Read the conversation between Gen and Sammi on page 36 of the *Student Book*. *Which place do you think will have the most pushes and pulls? Will it be more pushes or more pulls? Why?* Make a general prediction – you could take this as a simple show of hands and record it on the board.

What to do

Gen and Sammi carry out a survey of the two sites. They visit both and take pictures. You could count the pushes and pulls directly.

If you can't use a building site, then go to a contrasting site to the playground, for example the shopping mall.

What you need

- Digital camera.
- Permission for off school site visits.
- A clipboard to make notes.

What to check

Students will need to distinguish between the movement of machinery, and how the machinery moves other objects.

Look for forces in action: pushes, pulls, and instances where machines both push and pull.

⚠️ Follow school guidelines for taking students offsite and related risk assessments.

Warn students against trespassing on building sites. Are building sites safe places? They may be for the work force, protected by hard hats and following safety rules. But trespassers can be in danger; this is a good moment to teach about these risks, and to point out that some risks (falling, being run over or crushed) are due to the huge forces in action on a building site.

Differentiation

More able students may be able to name many of the machines and describe their movements related to the forces (pushes and pulls) involved.

What did you find?

The answer to the question here is going to depend highly on what the students actually found when they went to the sites. Gen and Sammi found that there were about the same number of pushes and pulls in both places.

Record

The results will be coloured onto the pictures taken, but these could be transferred onto block graphs with four columns, one each for pushes and pulls in each place.

Did you know?

Machines are devices to make work easier.

Other ideas

WS 15

- Look at *Student Book* page 37 again. What would you like in your own push/pull playground? Design a push/pull playground for the class. Make it either a whole class activity, with each student providing one illustrated idea for the playground; or a group activity with small groups working on large pieces of paper. Complete WS 15.

- Let students tell or write a story entitled, 'My visit to the playground', based on their work on the push/pull playground.

Plenary

- Model the movement of machines through drama. Using all the words for movement that the students identified with the building site machines and ask them to move in a similar way. Put the students into pairs. One is the machine, the other is the object that is to be moved. They are acting out their roles and that there is no need for them to lift each other. Give them time to practise and then show their movement pieces to the rest of the class.

- Set up a reward system for every time someone uses the word 'push' or 'pull' in class. This highlights how many forces are around us all the time!

New International Edition

Unit 4: Forces – How far can you go?

The objectives for this lesson are that students should be able to:

- Understand that the amount of force applied to an object affects how far it moves

- Take part in an investigation on force and movement

- Make predictions on what will happen

- Record and share their results.

SB pp.38–39

Starter

- Sit students in a circle to roll a ball to each other, calling out the student's name to pass it to. Go faster, calling out the names of things to push. The ball will generally be less accurate and will travel further as they push it harder.

- Display several toy cars of different shapes, sizes, materials, etc. and discuss how they could be grouped. Suggestions may include: colour, shape, size, type of wheel, material, streamlined, name. *Which of the cars might travel the furthest? Why? How could you test them to find out?* List their ideas and then let them choose one to test.

The challenge

Share the conversation that the children are having on *Student Book* page 38 about whose car is going the furthest and how they are doing it. Ask them to model with cars on the floor. Say that you aren't quite sure you believe them and that they need to be scientific and to produce some results to show others that they are right.

What to do

Use a large space, for example a hall, and get ready to push a car along the floor. Ask students how far they think the car will go. Ask students to stand where they think the car will end up. How close were they?

Ask students how they could record how far the car went so that they can show proof to each other. This could be measured with non-standard measures, or photographs of the students standing in their predicted places and then the car where it stopped, or stickers marked on the floor and photographed, or even long strips of paper from a base line to show prediction in one colour and result in another colour.

Students should then explain what they have found out and what the marks on the floor or their measurements show.

What you need

- Range of cars in different colours, so students don't get confused about whose car is whose.

- Something to mark the floor or measure distance.

- Digital camera.

What to check

The students should consider where to start their push from and where to measure from for 'fairness'.

They will also need to be encouraged to accept if they guess wrong about how far the cars travel. Younger students (and some more grown up ones!) like to be right!

> ⚠ Teach road safety rules.
>
> Toy cars left lying around can create a tripping or slipping hazard.

Differentiation

More able students may be able to use a metre stick or a trundle wheel to measure in standard units.

What did you find?

In general terms the harder the push the further the car should travel. This should be supported by the students' investigations and recording of the information.

Record

The activity could be extended to look at different types of cars, as well as the size of the push.

Make lots of blank thought bubbles for students to fill in whenever they want to and to share their ideas about different cars, for example 'I think the plastic car would not go very far because the wheels do not go round very well.' Display the bubble as a backdrop to the car collection.

Let students record their investigation activity in a zig-zag book. Head each section to allow students to sequence their recording, for example 'First we...', 'Then we...', 'After that we...', 'We noticed that...'. Let students share their books with the whole class.

Did you know?

For its size the dung beetle is one of the strongest animals on Earth as it can move so much. It would be the same as a grown man moving a railway engine of about 65 tonnes!

Plenary

- Ask the students to predict what will happen if you push a ball really hard across the floor. Use other objects to establish that the harder you push, the further the object travels.

New International Edition

Unit 4: Forces – Slow down

The objectives for this lesson are that students should be able to:

- Learn how to make something speed up and slow down

- Understand the dangers of speeding and stopping something

- Explain how going too fast might cause an accident

- Communicate, using units of speed.

SB p.40

Starter

- Remind students that they have already discussed keeping safe in school. Sometimes, moving things outside school can be dangerous to us. Discuss cars and other vehicles on the roads and how long it takes them to stop.

- Use two wooden trolleys, or something that can be pushed, with pillows strapped to the front and run them into one another, or into a wall and look at the change in shape at different speeds, walking and running.

Explain

Students may well 'understand' faster and slower. They may use speeds in km/hr without understanding them. The calculation of speed and the concepts are covered much later in science, but the awareness is here at this level.

Ouch!

Many students may have fallen over when going too fast. Discuss how this feels and how they made themselves go faster, for example pushing harder on the pedals of a bike or on the ground next to a skateboard.

⚠️ Teach road safety rules.

Things to do

Reinforce that the harder the push (the bigger the force), the further the car will go, and the harder the impact will be.

Roll large toy cars into blocks of soft, pliable Plasticine at different speeds. Use increasingly harder pushes to roll the cars.

- *How does the speed affect the impression left in the Plasticine?*

- *What does this tell us about what happens when cars crash at speed?*

- *Is this test fair?*

The activity could be made fairer by using a ramp to roll the cars down, rather than relying on a variable push. Try this instead and compare results with the first attempts. Save the Plasticine from each run. Use a digital camera to photograph the dents.

As an alternative, let students roll a toy car into a small block and see how far the block is moved each time. Mark the distance the block moves with ribbons or strips of paper. Convert the ribbons/strips into a bar chart to provide a visual comparison. Or record the damage to a wall made from toy bricks.

Differentiation

When investigating a car crashing into a block, students could measure the distance the block moves and record their results in a table. They could use centimetre cubes to build a graph; then copy the cubes on to centimetre squared paper to make a bar chart.

When looking at the road safety materials, some students could order pictures and sentences. More able students may be able to create and order their own sentences.

Did you know?

A fast car not only will hurt you more, but will stop later. You can model this with students running from A to B and being asked to stop suddenly and then being asked to stop from walking. Doing this on push bikes works well too.

Dig deeper

The fastest animal on land is the cheetah. The spine-tailed swift is the fastest bird at 170 kph (kilometres per hour). A peregrine falcon is the fastest bird in a headlong dive. They can travel up to 322 kph! (But they have gravity to help them.)

I wonder...

Commercial aeroplanes travel at about 967 kph, but military jets can go faster than the speed of sound, which is 1236 kph.

Other ideas

- Encourage students to consider their own safety on the roads. Read road safety leaflets and books.

- Put a teddy in a brick truck. *What will happen if the truck crashes into a wall?* Crash the truck and see what happens to teddy. Make teddy an elastic band seat belt and crash the truck again. *How did the seat belt help? How do they help in real car crashes?* Let students use a digital camera to record how well teddy fares with and without a seat belt.

- Consider other factors that affect how far a vehicle will go before it stops. Roll an empty brick truck down a ramp and see how far it goes. Add some bricks and try again. *How does the weight of the truck affect how far it goes?*

- Set up a car with a string and a mass attached. Hang the mass over the end of the table so the car moves when it is let go. *How can you make the car go faster and slower?*

Presentation

Ask students to devise their own set of road safety rules. Present these in an assembly. Devise a short drama to highlight the dangers of roads. Demonstrate how to cross roads safely.

Plenary

WS 16

- Use WS 16 to consolidate learning.

- Ask the students to link the force of the push with the distance and the speed of travel.

Unit 4: Forces – Other ways of moving things

The objectives for this lesson are that students should be able to:

- Find out how to move objects without touching them

- Observe how air and water can move objects

- Record and explain the force of air or water

- Share and communicate their results.

Starter
(SB p.41)

- Challenge students to make a piece of paper move without touching it. How do they do it?

- Look out of the window on a windy day. *Can you see anything moving that is being pushed by the wind?* Ask the students to act out how to walk in very strong winds or draw a picture of themselves in the wind.

- Use a film clip from the beginning of *The Wizard of Oz* where the tornado lifts up Dorothy's house, or show a film clip of the wind in action.

Explain

Some students think that blowing is different from other moving air because it has come from inside them.

Is the wind invisible?

Take the students out to experience any wind. Spot the wind effects. *How do we know it's a windy day? What can you see? What are the good effects of the wind? What can be the bad effects?*

Water wheels

Let students experience using sand and water (separately) to move things, for example with sand/water wheels. Students should put their hands in the flowing water and sand to feel the pushing force. They can record these activities.

Digital photographs of the activities could be included with the records.

> ⚠️ When making paper windmills you should supervise students pushing drawing pins into dowel rods.

Things to do

- Encourage using the phrase 'pushing force' to reinforce that movement is made by something other than themselves.

- Make paper windmills. Spin them outside in the wind. Blow on them to make them spin. *What made the windmill move?* Question them on the strength of blow/wind compared to the speed of turning.

- Carry out a safe investigation into who has the biggest puff and can make the windmill go round the fastest.

- Use the windmills to see where the wind is strongest around the school.

Differentiation

If some students use pictures to record their reports, an adult can scribe the writing next to the pictures.

Did you know?

A hurricane can have winds travelling in excess of 200 kilometres per hour (125 mph). Discuss how strong winds and floods can devastate people's lives. What can students find out about hurricanes, tornadoes, floods and tidal waves? *How do these affect people's lives?*

Dig deeper

The movement of the sails on a windmill drives a generator that converts movement energy into electrical energy. Some bicycles have a dynamo to generate electricity without batteries when you pedal.

I wonder...

Water turbines convert movement energy into electrical energy through a dynamo.

Explain the benefits of strong forces of wind and water. In the past, windmills and watermills were used to grind flour or power tools. Now they generate electricity.

Other ideas

WS 17

- In pairs, sitting opposite each other, let students play a 'blow football' game using straws and ping-pong balls. See who can blow the ball harder. Provide simple goals to make the activity into a game.

> ⚠ The blow football activity may not be appropriate for students with asthma or other breathing difficulties.

- *What classroom items can you move by blowing at them through a straw?* Choose five things to try. What do they think will happen? Try it out. Were they right? *What is the biggest thing you can blow with a straw?*

- Look at ways of sheltering from the wind with sheets and windbreaks, like those used on the beach.

- Make a weatherwave to look at the direction that wind travels, using WS 17.

Presentation

Set up a tournament for blow football.

Read Aesop's fable *The Sun and the North Wind*, and discuss whether the North Wind or the Sun is the stronger. Let students act out the fable. Illustrate the story of *The Sun and the North Wind.*

Plenary

- Talk about ways of observing and measuring the wind in action.

- Devise some simple 'wind measures' – tissue streamers on a stick, a hanging sheet of card or some yoghurt pots on arms, rotating on a bearing, can all qualitatively measure wind speed.

- Ask a challenging question: *How can we help a sailing boat to get across a lake? Can we change the boat in any way to make it easier for it to move across the lake?*

- *The Sun and the North Wind* in Aesop's fables allows students to discuss whether the North Wind or the Sun is stronger, and recognize that the North Wind is providing a force when it is trying to blow the coat off the man.

95

Unit 4: Forces – Which way next?

The objectives for this lesson are that students should be able to:

- Understand how to make moving things change direction

- Recognize that push or pull forces are needed

- Safely take part in experiments on changing direction

- Follow and give instructions on how and when to change direction.

SB p.42

Starter

- In the hall play some running games and shout out directions.

- *What do you have to do to change direction? If you are by a wall is this easier or harder?*

Explain

> Students with asthma and other breathing difficulties should not over-exert themselves blowing balls or boats.
>
> Ensure any electrical equipment has been tested for safety prior to use.

Things to do

- Use a large football to roll across the floor and ask students to push it towards each other. How do they do it? Can they make it change direction without touching it?

- Provide small balls or ping pong balls and a range of paper straws, hair driers, etc. *Imagine the ball is coming towards you. You want to make it travel in a different direction. What will you do to it?* The students will have to first 'stop' the ball then make it move in a direction they want.

- Use small trikes or cars for students to push or pull each other along. *How do they go round corners?*

Differentiation

The concept of change of direction is hard as forces can't be seen but can only be felt. Try to ensure that children struggling with this concept get a chance, to feel direction-changing forces directly. For example by placing a student on a wheeled chair and pushing them and then changing their direction they may experience it from the object's point of view. Pushing each other they can then better feel the forces needed.

Did you know?

Not only do you almost stop when you change direction, but you also have to push against something. Swimmers touch the sides of the pool. Runners may push against a wall if there is one, or put a foot at an angle to push against the floor – try it and see.

Dig deeper

Bicycles and scooters change direction because the rider applies push and pull forces to the handlebars. The vehicle follows the direction of the steered wheel.

I wonder...

An aeroplane can't turn suddenly as it pushes against the air. Many students don't believe that air is 'something'.

Other ideas

- Make model sailboats and use a straw to blow them across a bowl of water. *What do you have to do to make the boat change direction?* Produce an obstacle course for the boat.

- Use a battery driven hand fan and explore the difference between the 'wind' speed and the movement of the boat.

- Create an obstacle course for dribbling a football. Encourage students to call out the instructions to go round it using as many forces words as possible.

Presentation

Produce a set of simple instructions on how to change an object's direction.

Demonstrate to another class how to change the direction of a ball, a car and a runner.

Plenary

- List all the forces needed to travel from your desk to the back of the classroom.

- Race boats around a course using only a straw to move them. Students then draw the course and mark where they have to blow from to change the boat's direction.

New International Edition

Unit 4: Forces – Blow football

The objectives for this lesson are that students should be able to:

- Learn how to make something change direction

- Plan and take part in the 'Blow football' game

- Communicate their ideas and discuss any problems

- Explain the 'Blow football' game rules and the forces used in it to younger students or each other.

SB p.43

Starter

- Explain that the players have to get a ball around a slalom course before a sand timer runs out.

- Discuss what a slalom course is. Show the picture on *Student Book* page 43 of the game being played.

Explain

Provide opportunities for students to share their ideas and problems before they make the game.

> ⚠ Students with asthma and other breathing difficulties should not over-exert themselves.

Things to do

As individuals or in pairs, encourage students to draw a plan of their game. Help them to think about the positions of the poles so that the players will have to change the push force to slow down, speed up and change the direction of the ball.

Devise a set of rules as a class. This will keep them simple. List them and ask students to go over them until they are happy that the rules are clear. Ask them to consider:

- *What forces should be used?*

- *What happens when someone reaches the end of the course?*

- *Do players have to reach the end before the sand timer runs out?*

- *What happens if the ball goes off the board? Is it a penalty? Do they have to start again?*

Have a 'slalom' competition with students playing against a timer. Let a student commentate on the game, using as much forces vocabulary as possible, for example 'And here she comes, pushing the ball between the poles. Now she is changing direction and finally a big push towards the finishing line.'

Differentiation

Support students in creating the game and encouraging them to talk through their ideas before they make it and solve the problem.

Less able students may need support to plan and make their game. Ask less able students to explain the forces used in their game.

More able students should be able to visualize and create their game with less supervision and will be able to create their own set of instructions. Challenge them to use statements like, 'If you want to make the ball slow down you will need to …'.

Did you know?

Footballers constantly vary the force and direction that they kick a ball. *How do other sports use forces?*

Dig deeper

Forces play a part in all physical sports.

I wonder...

Even writing uses a force, as you push on the paper with the pen or pencil. You then push the pencil across the page. You pull pages when you turn a book. You pull a chair out and push it in.

Other ideas

- Look at a range of games, books and puppets that use forces, for example blow football games, Pickup Sticks, marbles, badminton, tennis rackets, bubbles. Ask students to demonstrate and talk about the forces that they use.

- Video the students presenting their game as the new 'must have' or as part of a sports programme with competitors, and them explaining the rules.

- Ask students to write the instructions for the 'slalom' game as a leaflet or zig-zag book with one instruction per page.

- Show students the 'domino' effect where dominoes are set up in a row so that when one is knocked over the rest fall in succession. What other chain reactions can they set up?

Presentation

Play the 'Blow football' game with students from another class.

Display the zig-zag books.

Time each other through the slalom and display them as a leader board.

Plenary

- Ask students how they could develop the game and try out their own ideas. They might make card bridges, for example to make a game like croquet. They might cut up parcel tube to make hoops for the ball to go through. They might race, with two balls at once on the board. As they develop the game, they will be putting forces into action.

- Ask students to explain to younger children how to use their game.

- Can students explain the forces used in the game in their written instructions?

New International Edition

Unit 4: Forces – Unit 4 Review

The objectives for this lesson are that students should be able to:

- Check what they have learned about forces in this Unit

- Find out how they are working towards, within and beyond the Grade 1 level.

SB p.44 | **Expectations**

Note: *items in italic are this Unit's scientific enquiry expectations.*

By the end of this Unit, students working towards Grade 1 will:

- observe and describe movements they and objects make

- describe how to make a familiar object start moving by pushing or pulling.

In addition, students working within Grade 1 level will:

- compare movements they make and movements of objects in terms of speed or direction

- describe how to use pushes and pulls to make familiar objects speed up, slow down, or change direction

- recognize dangers to themselves in moving objects

- recognize that pushes and pulls are forces

- *make measurements of length and compare these.*

Further to this, students working beyond Grade 1 level will also:

- describe how windmills or water wheels are made to move

- describe why it can be dangerous to try to stop a heavy object moving

- *plan a comparison and decide whether it was fair*

- *make measurements of length using standard units and present these in a chart.*

Check-up

Ask the students to explain how one of their games works. The students should use forces words to describe what they plan to do and why.

Assessment   WS 18

Use the Unit 4 assessment to check the students' understanding of the content of the Unit. The answers are given below.

Name: _____ Date: _____

WS 18   **Unit 4 Assessment**

1 Write or draw three things in the sets below.

Things I can push

Things I can push and pull

Things I can pull

2 Draw a circle around the right answer in each sentence.

a) When I push the car harder, it goes
   further   less far

b) When I push the car gently, it goes
   further   less far

18   Heinemann Explore Science Grade 1

Written assessment
Answers to Workbook WS 18, Unit 4 review

1   Answers will vary but may include:
   - Things I can push: wheelbarrow, doorbell, light switch, bicycle, bicycle pedal.
   - Things I can pull: rope, elastic band, sledge.
   - Things I can push and pull: a door, a drawer, a window, a gate.

2   **a**   When I push the car harder, it goes further.
    b   When I push the car gently, it goes less far.

The answer!

Could you get dressed if you could only push and not pull? (See page 33, Student Book)

Getting dressed as well as many simple, everyday tasks would be impossible.

And finally...

Create a display of objects that can be pushed, pulled or both. This could be in the form of a Venn diagram with intersecting sets.

Zig-zag books look good on a display board – they can be left standing out to give the display a 3D effect of information on pushes and pulls.

The bar charts created using strips of paper/ribbons look effective when displayed and can be referred to when concluding what happened in the investigation.

A wall display of a building site can include key vocabulary of movement in a relevant context.

Put together a large wall display based on a circus, with jugglers throwing pins, clowns pushing each other over, an acrobat falling into a safety net, clowns on a trampoline, etc. Include questions such as:

- Where can you see a push force?
- Where is someone changing the direction of something?
- How many pull forces can you see being used?
- Where do you think the biggest push force is? Why?

A similar display could be made of a children's playground with swings, slides, roundabouts and sea-saws.

A table-top interactive display could include toys that can move, be pushed, pulled, can change shape, etc. Include a set of questions or suggestions for the students to do, for example: Sort the toys into two groups that can be pushed or pulled. Which toys can be squeezed to change their shape? Which toys can change direction?

New International Edition

Unit 5: Sound

The objectives for this Unit are that students should be able to:

- Identify many sources of sound

- Know that sounds are heard when they enter the ear

- Recognize that as sound travels from a source it becomes fainter.

SB pp.45–56   *Science background*

We live in a world of sounds – naturally occurring sounds such as a crash of thunder, birds singing and people speaking, as well as artificially made noise such as the roar of traffic. 'Noise' is usually used to refer to unpleasant sounds. We combine sounds in rhythms and melodies to make music. Sound is one of the most basic ways of communicating for some animals.

Children are very good at making different sounds, often the loudest sounds possible, and they need encouragement to listen for quiet sounds. They need practice in distinguishing high and low sounds as well as identifying the direction of sounds.

How sound is made

Sound is all around us, but what is it? You can't see it. Sound originates as vibration. The energy of this vibration is transferred to the air as a pressure wave, spreading out as an expanding sphere. Sound waves alternately squeeze (compress) and stretch (rarefy) the air or material through which they pass, causing the molecules to collide.

Sound waves can be contained. For instance, if you speak down a long piece of tubing, the tube prevents the sound waves from spreading out and allows them to travel over a long distance.

Sound waves can be magnified. Bang a drum or pluck a string and they vibrate, sending waves of energy through the air. A sound box amplifies the sound.

Sound travels as a longitudinal wave. This is difficult to show, except with a slinky spring, as the particles only move in one plane – backwards and forwards – passing the energy on in the direction of the sound. Pull a horizontal slinky spring gently backwards and watch the movement along its length (don't wave it up and down). The coils bump into each other, knocking each one forward in turn. Vibrations or colliding particles travel through the air (or other materials – liquids and solids) to reach our ears. The waves make our eardrums vibrate and messages are sent to the brain, which then makes sense of them so that we identify sounds.

- Sounds can be naturally (such as the wind whistling in the trees) or artificially produced (such as an emergency siren).

- Some sounds are quiet while others are loud. This is called the loudness or volume.

- Some are high and others low. This is called the pitch.

It can be harder to identify what is making an actual sound and where it is coming from if we cannot see the source. As our lives are full of noise, children are often poor at listening carefully. Closing their eyes can help them concentrate on developing their listening skills.

Speed of sound

The speed of sound does not affect its loudness or pitch. All sound travels at the same speed in the same material at the same temperature (otherwise all the sounds of instruments in an orchestra would reach your ears at different times and the music would be jumbled).

Sound travels through air at 340 metres per second at 20 degrees Celsius (it goes faster at higher temperatures, and slower at lower ones).

Sound travels at different speeds through different materials. It travels faster through water than through air (about five times faster), and even faster through solids (20 times faster).

Sounds must travel through something – in outer space where there is no air there are no sounds. Light travels one million times faster than sound. This is why you see lightning before you hear the accompanying thunder clap. Unlike light, which travels in a straight line from a source, sound spreads out in all directions so you hear it all around you. Like light, sounds diminish as they travel away f rom their source.

Sound as music

Sounds can be linked together in ways to create rhythms and music. Patterns of sound can be written down as notes and read in the same way that we read words on a page. Young students can practise clapping and copying repeating patterns as an early introduction to music.

In order to make a sound, something has to vibrate or move. This could be your vocal cords, or the air vibrating inside a recorder. The shorter or faster the vibration, the higher the pitch. Thin, tight strings on a guitar sound higher than thick, looser ones. To make effective music the sounds need to be amplified (made louder) so that we can hear them. A box of air amplifies the sound and spreads it out in all directions. This is why guitars, cellos and drums have a big body. The sound can be further amplified electronically.

Ears

Our ears are the sense organs of hearing. The outer ear is funnel-shaped to focus and collect the sound more effectively. Ear trumpets work this way. Within the ear is the eardrum – a delicate skin that vibrates when a sound wave hits it. These vibrations are carried into the ear by a series of little bones to the fluid in the inner ear. This causes tiny hairs on nerves to move, sending electrical messages to the brain to interpret. (Don't attempt to teach the structure of the ear. But point out that the sense organs are inside our heads. Students may think that the ear just consists of a flap and a hole!) Other animals have more pronounced outer ears than humans. For instance, many prey animals have large mobile ears that enable them to pick up the small sounds of approaching predators. Many predators have forward-facing ears that help them accurately locate their prey. Elephants have big ears which they use to keep them cool. Animals that make a sound can also be expected to have ears – even if they don't have earflaps. Frogs have eardrums on the sides of their head. Grasshoppers and crickets have ears on their knees and they rub their legs on their wings to make a chirping sound.

Humans hear a far narrower range of sounds than many animals. We can hear sounds that vibrate between 20–18 000 times each second. Killer whales can hear up to 100 000 vibrations per second. Dogs can hear high-pitched sounds that humans cannot detect at all.

Purposes of sounds

Many animals use sound as a way of warning other animals. The roar of a tiger can be heard over 3 km away. Loud, high-pitched sounds which attract our attention (e.g. sirens, alarm bells, whistles) are often used to signal danger. Speech and hearing are the main forms of human communication. Other sense organs often become more highly developed in people who have hearing limitations or no voice and they use alternative communication systems including sign language, lip reading and speech synthesis.

Loudness and safety

The loudness of sounds is measured in decibels (dB). The decibel scale is not linear – 20 dB is not twice as loud as 10 dB – and is best avoided at this stage. Sounds over 120 dB can cause intense pain and possible deafness. The loudness of a sound is determined by the size of vibrations produced.

> ⚠ It is essential in any work on sound that students do not make loud sounds close to the eardrum or push any objects into their ears (they risk permanent damage to their hearing as the eardrum is very delicate).

Language

Ear The sense organ we use for hearing.

Eardrum A delicate skin that vibrates transferring sound waves into the inner ear.

Hearing The way we make sense of sounds through our ears.

Pictogram A graph where each picture represents a separate piece of data.

Pitch The frequency of a sound (high or low) determined by the speed of the vibrations.

Sound A vibration received and interpreted by the brain; what we hear.

Vibration A rapid movement of particles in a material (gas, solid or liquid).

Volume The loudness of a sound caused by the amount of vibrations.

Wave The vibration of air particles in the same direction as the sound is travelling.

Key vocabulary

The following words might be introduced or used with the children alongside others, to accustom them to the nature of scientific vocabulary:

communicate	investigate
compare	measure
describe	observe
discover	record
explore	test
interpret	

These words may be of use in terms of comparisons:

distant	low
direction	music
echo	quiet
faint	sensing
high	soft
instruments	sound effects
listening	source of sound
loud	speaking

Resources

A full list of resources is located at the start of the *Teacher's Book* for ease of gathering resources. Many resources will already be in the classroom, but a few may need prior arrangement. For example:

- Tape recorder or CD player.

- A range of materials for making sound effects (greaseproof paper, plastic bags, sand or pebbles in a bottle, musical instruments, whistles, bells or sirens).

- Recordings of different sounds, including animal noises.

- Music tapes/CDs including Benjamin Britten's *Young Person's Guide to the Orchestra* and Prokofiev's *Peter and the Wolf*.

- A range of different musical instruments – tuned and untuned percussion, wind and string as well as ones from different cultures.

- Pictures of different animals' ears.

- Blindfolds.

- Earmuffs.

- Alarm clocks.

- A piece of flexible tube (such as a garden or vacuum cleaner hose).

- The reader *Sound and Hearing* may be used with this Unit.

Bright ideas

- Explore the percussion instruments in school. Sort them into untuned percussion (such as drums, cymbals, triangles) and tuned percussion (such as xylophone, metallophone). *What materials are these made from? How does holding a cymbal or triangle in your hand change the sound, deadening it? Does the same thing happen if you hold the xylophone keys? Will the keys work away from the frame? Why not?*

- Sound boxes amplify sounds. Look for sound boxes on musical instruments in school. Explore the effects of sound boxes by making a simple one-string 'guitar' – a taut string between the ends of a curved stick. Twang it. Then place an inflated balloon between the string and the stick, and twang again. The balloon acts as a sound box.

- *Does sound go up and down, as well as around in all directions?* Think of everyday examples of hearing sounds from above (such as passing aeroplanes) and below (such as calls from downstairs). Try it out if you can safely get above and below a sound source.

Knowledge check

Students should develop their knowledge of their sense of hearing and understand that we hear sounds through our ears (building on Unit 1 *Ourselves and other animals*).

Skills check

Students need to:

- practise listening carefully, locating, describing and recording sounds.

- be able to recognize many different sources and kinds of sounds.

- discover different ways of making sounds and appreciate when sounds become music.

- learn that all sounds result from vibrations and that they can be naturally and artificially produced.

- know that sounds are heard when they enter the ear.

- appreciate the dangers of loud sounds, and how hearing helps keep us safe.

Some students will:

- investigate how sounds travel in different directions and diminish with distance.

Students will use observation, description and communication skills, and record their findings with simple pictures, words and tables.

Links to other subjects

Literacy: Speak and listen, including recordings. Identify sound patterns. Distinguish between every day and scientific language. Name sounds. Develop descriptive words for sounds. Follow simple instructions. Read fiction (stories and rhymes). Use information books. Take part in group discussions.

Numeracy: Count and identify repeating patterns in other contexts.

Describe and extend sequences. Communicate using symbols. Measure, record and present data.

Music: The science of sounds links strongly to Music (using voices, playing tuned and untuned percussion instruments, creating musical patterns, organizing sounds and making them in different ways, using music to express ideas and feelings).

Making musical instruments links to design-and-make activities in design and technology, and decoration work can be linked to art and design.

ICT: Students can use ICT in recording and playing back sounds as well as working with specialist computer programs such as *Music Maker Pitch* (Resource).

Let's find out...

This Unit opens with the questions:

What if we lived on a planet without any words? How else could we use sounds?

Sounds can evoke a range of feelings and emotions and pictures by association. These questions will help check understanding of this, but also they are an ongoing challenge for faster workers.

Unit 5: Sound – Sounds all around

The objectives for this lesson are that students should be able to:

- Use their sense of hearing to explore and identify sounds

- Understand that there are many sources and types of sound

- Recognize and describe many different sounds

- Write a class or individual poem using descriptive words for sound.

SB p.46   Starter

- Sit on a whoopy cushion to elicit a response from the students. *Who made the sound? What did it sound like? Was it a nice noise? Can you repeat it?*

- Let students investigate the sounds they can make with different parts of their bodies (prepare for some rude noises!). They can clock and clap, stamp, sniff and blow, and hum, whistle, speak and sing. *Can you make any sounds with your eyes or ears? Why not?* Ask the students to describe the sounds.

Explain

Students with hearing difficulties will need extra help.

Ask students how they know there are sounds around them. Draw out that they hear with their ears – recapping the topics about ourselves.

Our senses

Remind students of the five senses.

Who is it?

Discuss how each sound we hear is unique. *Can you tell who calls you? Can you tell if they are happy? How?*

> ⚠ Warn students about the dangers of loud noises and putting objects in the ear.

Things to do

Identify your friends

Blindfold a student in the middle of a circle. Can they identify other students from the sounds they make with their bodies? *Is it harder when the sounds are quiet and easier when they are loud?*

- Let students predict before trying.

- Record the results in a simple table: 'Peter whistles loudly; Anne points to him'.

A sound poem

Write down all the descriptive words for the sounds and turn them into a poem, by writing them in threes and saying them in a hushed voice.

Choose the favourite class descriptive word and use this as a repeating chorus for every line. The students can then try their own poems.

Differentiation

Let more able students listen for difference in the voices of different aged people.

- *Are there differences between young and old students?*

- *Between child and adult voices?*

- *Between male and female?*

Did you know?

You can prove this to students with a couple of short activities.

- Feel your throat as you hum. *Can you feel the vibrations?* Set up a radio and feel the loudspeaker playing, in turn.

- Twang a ruler over the side of a table. *Can you see the vibrations?* Allow students to experience the vibrations before you provide the word. Allow the students to describe what they feel in their own words, this may be 'fizzing' or 'wobbling'.

- Lightly hold an inflated balloon with your fingertips. Speak against it – the balloon will vibrate with each sound, just as an eardrum does.

Dig deeper

Some students may be aware that people can be born deaf. Loud noises can make you temporarily deaf as they desensitize your ears. Generally this is quickly repaired by the body, but constant loud noise can damage your ears permanently.

I wonder...

Explore what it might be like if you had a hearing problem by wearing a scarf around your ears, or wearing earmuffs. Discuss the things they would miss. These might include music, the sounds of nature and people's voices. If people can't communicate, they might be lonely.

Remind students of their sense lessons and how deaf people 'talk' to each other. Invite an expert to demonstrate sign language and lip reading.

Learn some simple messages in sign language. Make a display of the most common signs.

Other ideas

- Unseen, make some familiar sounds. Ask students to identify them by drawing pictures. In turn, let students make different sounds for others to identify.

- Record familiar and less familiar sounds for students to listen to. Include a washing machine, a zip opening, animal noises, the roar of busy traffic or a police siren. (Closing their eyes while listening will help to improve concentration.) Ask students to identify each sound with a picture: *Where might you hear that sound? Who or what makes that noise?*

Presentation

Act out a role-play using sound effects, or record a story with appropriate sound effects.

Display poems and stories that incorporate sounds.

Plenary

- Create a wall mural and add labels of descriptive words for sounds such as 'plop', 'ping', 'click', 'squeak'.

- List all the words associated with sound. Try and find descriptive words that are like the sound (onomatopoeia) and display these.

- Create a role-play situation where students are invited into a 'recording studio' one at a time. They are not told what sound to make until they are in front of the microphone. Challenge them to make a sound in different ways: with their feet, their hair, the table, or with a pencil. Record each in turn. Then play the tape back. Can the class remember which sound was which?

- *Imagine being in space where there is no sound. How would you communicate?* (Light and radio waves travel through a vacuum.)

Unit 5: Sound – Where is quietest?

The objectives for this lesson are that students should be able to:

- Make predictions about where the quietest place might be

- Listen for and make a record of sounds around the school

- Make a visual representation of their findings as a map

- Record their findings in a graph.

SB pp.47–48 — Starter

- Ask the children to listen to *The Carnival of the Animals* (1886), a piece of music by composer Camille Saint-Saëns, and to decide which animal is being described by the music. Turn the volume up quite loud (but not dangerously!)

- Put your hands over your ears and ask how we can make it quieter. Turn the volume down and try again. The music for the elephant which is only about 1 minute long is a good one to start with. Compare this to the aquarium or the hens and chickens pieces.

The challenge

Share how the teacher on page 47 of the *Student Book* has a headache as her class have been very noisy. She needs to find a quiet place to concentrate and have a cup of tea.

Ask the children where they think the quietest place in school will be and why, for example no-one else is in there.

What to do

Discuss how you could find the quietest place in the school and be able to prove your results. You need to be able to record them.

Ask the students where the sounds are coming from. This is the source of the sound.

Take a group on a sound walk around school. *What sounds can you hear? How can you record them?*

Listen carefully for natural sounds such as the wind, birds singing or dogs barking. Count the number of different sounds heard in one area and record these. Using a tape recorder can help to check these when back in the classroom.

How many sounds can students remember back in the classroom?

Transfer the numbers onto a map of the school, so there is a visual representation.

What you need

- Clipboard.

- Tape recorder.

- Images of things that make sounds around the schools, cut-out into small squares.

What to check

Ensure that the students are listening carefully and not just being subjective, saying somewhere is quiet or noisy and not qualifying it with data.

⚠️ Take care with loud sounds.

More able students could write the actual sounds down that were heard.

Look at page 48 and discuss the results that the teacher found.

Students could produce a block graph of these results as well as answer the questions posed in the book.

Record

Use a table similar to that shown in the *Student Book* to record the sounds.

Turn the results into a simple block graph. This can be an abstract task for students, by having an image of the things making the sounds, for example children, birds, cars, instruments, laughing face, shouting face, feet for footsteps, etc.

Use this to mark the blocks on the chart. Discuss what this shows and whether this makes it easier to decide which is noisiest and quietest than the table. Establish that a chart or graph is a visual representation of the table.

The Blue Whale can make sounds with a single click that are louder than our ears can stand. Humans can just about cope with 120 dB (decibels), but the Blue Whale makes a sound at about 188 dB.

- Discuss the need for quiet and loud sounds.
- Play the original music quieter this time and ask students to act out the animal they think the music is representing. The swan is another good piece to play. Discuss whether it was easier to hear the quieter or louder music.

Unit 5: Sound – Music makers

The objectives for this lesson are that students should be able to:

- Recognize musical instruments and explain what sounds they make

- Find out how to make sounds using instruments they have made

- Consider how to make sounds louder or quieter

- Take part in a concert using the instruments they made.

SB p.49 | *Starter*

- Listen to Benjamin Britten's *Young Person's Guide to the Orchestra* or Prokofiev's *Peter and the Wolf* to identify sounds made by different instruments.

- Listen carefully and call out names of instruments played, or point to them on the board.

Explain

Encourage appreciation of different types of music and ways of expressing feelings through music.

Anticipate confusion between loud and soft, and high and low.

Crash, bang, wallop

Look at *Student Book* page 49. Name the instruments. Ask the students what sorts of sounds they make.

Discuss whether any students already play a musical instrument and how they get a note from it. Ask them to demonstrate if they can.

Make your own

Develop students' practical skills in the making activities, focusing on appearance as well as purpose.

Make a range of simple musical instruments – stretch elastic bands over an empty tissue box to make a 'guitar'; stretch a plastic bag tightly over a bowl to make a 'drum'; wave a piece of heavy card to make a wobble-board; make a scraper with a sandpaper block; make a xylophone by putting different amounts of water in glass bottles and tapping them in turn. Make a drinking straw recorder with paper straws. Flatten the end where you blow and cut at an angle on both corners. Cut the straw shorter and shorter between each blow.

Ask students to name them or match them to school instruments.

> ⚠ Be careful with elastic bands stretched too tightly, and with plastic bags.

Things to do

- *How will you get a sound out of the instruments? Which do you strike, pluck, scrape, shake or blow?* Let students see what sounds they can produce from a range of musical instruments, include percussion and recorders. Demonstrate a couple and ask the students how they made the sound.

- Compare the instruments shown with the school's instruments. Ask students to group these, according to how the sounds are made.

- Make a set of panpipes using drinking straws of diminishing length held together with sticky tape. What do students notice as they blow across the top of the straws?

- Make a range of other instruments. For example, make shakers by putting pulses, etc. in a screw-top plastic bottle or by securely sticking two yoghurt pots together. What different sounds can they make with different contents?

- Ask the students how they can change the sound made by the instrument, for example make it louder or quieter.

Differentiation

More able students can use electronic devices for making sounds. *How do the sounds differ from actual instruments? Can you copy the beats or rhythms? Can you write simple symbols to represent the rhythm?*

Did you know?

When nails are scraped down a board they can make us shiver because we don't like sounds we can't easily predict. We don't know where the sound is going next, which makes us feel uncomfortable.

Dig deeper

The answer to this may well depend on how hard the drum is played. The drums can be very loud but then so can a member of the brass section!

I wonder...

Some people wear aids to enhance their hearing. They may be worn in or behind their ears. Often they make use of the bone conduction of sound.

Other ideas

- Investigate different materials that make loud and quiet sounds. Tap a piece of wood, metal, leather, a plastic tray, a sponge and a stone. *Which sound is loud? Which sound is quiet or soft?*

- Sort the materials into two groups. *Can some make both loud and soft sounds? Does it depend on the beater and how hard you tap?*

- Wrap a hard beater in cotton wool. *Does it make a difference?*

Presentation

Hold a concert in which everyone plays an instrument they have made.

Make and hang up wind chimes. Ask how they work.

Plenary

WS 19

- Invite a musician to play a range of instruments in the classroom.

- Can students predict what sort of sound an instrument will make, for example ting, toot, crash, twang, hum, etc? WS 19 can help with this.

- Can they predict how they can get an instrument to make a sound by looking at it? *What clues are there?* Ask students the names of some instruments.

- Listen to some melodic band or orchestral music without any singing. What instruments do students think are making the sounds? Do they like the music? What emotions does it conjure up? Now talk about the people making the music. *How are they doing it? How could they make music if they didn't have the instruments?*

Unit 5: Sound – All ears

The objectives for this lesson are that students should be able to:

- Explain why they need to listen carefully

- Investigate how sound travels and is made louder

- Find out about objects that enhance their hearing

- Research, using secondary sources, the first sound recordings made by Thomas Edison in 1877.

SB p.50

Starter

- Do students know that it is the nature of the sound or the distance that affects its volume, not their ears? Play a tape at different volumes and ask students to compare and describe the sounds.

- Play a game where whenever students hear a student behind them, they turn and pounce on them. Pretend to be different animals – gazelles can listen for lions approaching. Blindfold the gazelles to see how hard it is relying on hearing alone. Then let them turn to see the lions who are 'out' if they are seen moving.

Explain

Many students have the misconception that our ears have 'volume' controls rather than the source of the sound, for example. 'I can't shout so loud when my hands are over my ears.'

Danger Danger

Play a range of sirens from emergency vehicles and ask the students which type of emergency vehicle they recognize. Ask students to describe the features of emergency vehicles siren that make them effective.

Animal ears

Some animals' ears aren't only used to hear, for example elephants' ears help them to cool down in the heat of the Sun.

Draw the shapes of different animals' ears, such as large elephant ears, pointed rabbit ears. Trace silhouettes of animals showing the size and shape of their ears in relation to the rest of their body. Use the silhouettes in a shadow play with students adding sound effects.

Heinemann Explore Science

⚠ Ensure students know the reasons to stop, look and listen when crossing roads.

Take small groups of students to practise road safety.

Things to do

Are two ears better than one?

Challenge students to discover if two ears are better than one. Ask: 'Does using only one ear affect your sense of direction of sound?'

Sit in a circle. One person sits in the middle blindfolded, with some keys behind their back. One person in the circle has to collect the keys without being heard. If the person in the middle points at them (finds the direction) they have to swap places.

Do this first with one ear covered, then the other then with both ears open. *Which is more accurate?* In practice, there is little difference. Moving our heads, and our working ear, give us more information.

Road safety

Discuss the importance of using our ears to listen carefully when crossing the road or in other dangerous situations.

Investigate why wearing hoods or earphones affects our hearing. Then listen to a sound with and without earmuffs. Use different materials for earmuffs and compare them.

Differentiation

More able students can research echoes.

Did you know?

Put your ear to a table – *how clearly can you hear your fingers tapping?* (It will sound louder than normal.) This is because the particles in a solid like wood are very close together and the sound can travel further and faster. It's possible to hear sounds through the ground by pushing a knife into the earth and putting an ear to it.

Dig deeper

This reinforces the need for safety when we cross the road and how we need to listen for cars that we have perhaps not seen yet, as they are round the corner.

I wonder...

Sound travels in all directions from a source. It will bounce off objects (like a reflection) to travel to the ear so we can hear it.

Other ideas

- Make a sound tube from a long piece of flexible hose. Put a plastic funnel on each end. Hold it to your chest and listen to your heartbeat. Loop the tube – you will still hear but you won't see any light through it if you shine a torch in one end of the tube. Put a plastic funnel on one end of a shorter piece of tube to make a horn.

- The ends of trumpets, trombones and clarinets are funnel-shaped to help the sound spread out. The chamber of a guitar (or the tissue box in a home-made guitar) acts as an amplifier, making the sound louder. Let students find where the sound comes from on a television, computer or hi-fi system.

Presentation

Use information sources to find out about the first sound recordings by Thomas Edison in 1877. *How many ways can sound be recorded?* (Students may not be familiar with records, the forerunners to tapes and CDs and MP3 players). Produce a display of different recording devices.

Plenary

- Discuss why people with visual impairments rely heavily on sounds. *How do people with hearing problems know the telephone is ringing?*

- Ask students how they hear. *What are the other four senses? How can they make sounds louder?*

- Ask them to describe the dangers of not listening in certain situations such as crossing roads.

- *Imagine a planet where communication is through sounds rather than words.* Can students create a special language which they can use to communicate simple messages?

Unit 5: Sound – Is bigger better?

The objectives for this lesson are that students should be able to:

- Make predictions about which size ear will receive the most sound

- Record their results in a table or using images

- Examine their results to check whether their predictions were correct

- Use their results to explain why some animals have big ears.

SB pp.51–52   *Starter*

- Talk about how we hear. Can students listen better? Does it help if they close their eyes so they can concentrate? *Put your hands over your ears. How does that affect hearing?*

- You might show a range of hearing devices, for example trumpets, implants and small devices that fit into the ear. Discuss how technology has moved on from the ear trumpet.

- Make a yoghurt pot telephone from two yoghurt pots and a piece of string. Pierce the holes in advance and tie paper clips to the string to stop it pulling through. Hold the string taut. Do not put your fingers on the string. Speak softly into the pots. Discuss how they work.

The challenge

Read the challenge set on page 51 of the *Student Book*. Ask the students to make a prediction of which ear size they think will be best. Remind them of work done on the animals' ear sizes.

What to do

The students should try three different sizes of paper trumpets to mimic ears. These should be placed by the ear. Don't roll the cones so small at the 'pointed end' that they fit into the ear, or this could cause irritation.

Although the students don't need to plan a fair test, they should be encouraged to stand the same distance away from the sound source and to have the sound source the same each time. You should discuss with the students why this is 'fair'. *Is there anything else we should do to make the investigation fair?*

What you need

If you don't use a drum, then a constant volume of a sound played on a tape recorder or from the computer can be a substitute.

Thin card works better than paper in this activity as it holds its shape better. Stick the cones so that they don't keep unrolling.

Have paper ranging from A5 to A2 size if you can.

A sound meter would be a useful addition to this activity or the 'loudness' of sound will be purely subjective in this case.

What to check

Ensure that the students don't think that the volume of the sound is being changed.

> ⚠ Don't play the instruments (drum) too close to the ear or too loudly.

Differentiation

More able students could record the size of the paper rather than just: large, small and medium.

What did you find?

The pattern should be that the bigger the ear the louder the sound. *Is there a limit to the effective size of an ear trumpet?*

Record

Students could record in a table, or lay out their trumpets in order, using a blank axis to help, so producing a bar chart of the results – these could be photographed. For example, the bottom axis has 'loudness' written on it. This will encourage sequencing, and hopefully the pattern of the paper size to volume should be seen.

Did you know?

Some people have vestigial muscles which they can control to wiggle their ears. Other skills that some people have include raising one eyebrow and rolling their tongue.

Plenary

Revisit some of the animal ears from the previous session and ask the students which animals might hear best. Show a range of nocturnal animals and ask them why they have such big ears. Ask why they have such big eyes too.

Revisit the telephones from the starter and ask what sized yoghurt pots we should use. Make the telephones and test them.

Try using the funnels as megaphones. See how loud you can shout outside. *Why does this happen?* The trumpet focuses the sound in one direction.

Unit 5: Sound – Sounds far away

The objectives for this lesson are that students should be able to:

- Understand how sound changes with distance

- Use their senses and observation skills to identify the loudness and location of sounds

- Recognize that sound travels outwards in all directions

- Share and explain their findings.

Starter
(SB p.53)

- Explore prior ideas and question any thinking that suggests that sound only travels in one direction.

- *What loud sounds can be heard over very long distances?* Draw up a list and divide it into naturally-occurring sounds (thunder, dogs barking, etc.) and artificially-produced sounds (sirens, bells).

- *Which sounds are pleasant/unpleasant?*

Explain

Students may believe that sound only travels in one direction, rather than outward in all directions.

How loud?

Play a range of sounds. *Which is quiet, which loud?* Show the picture on *Student Book* page 53 and ask the students what they think each child can hear.

Sounds and safety

Talk about sounds that alert us to danger (sirens, etc). Many animals, such as dogs and cats, use sound as a warning. Brainstorm other warning sounds (oven timers, pedestrian crossing beeps, etc). *What do these sound have in common?* They are all high pitched. Students won't know about pitch at this stage, but will recognize 'high and low', possibly from music lessons.

> ⚠ Be aware of the dangers of loud sounds close to the ears.

Things to do

- Develop a word bank of descriptive and rhyming words related to sound.

- Take different sound sources to an open space, like the hall of a playground. Stand the students in a line that runs away from the sound source. If they raise their hands as they can hear the sound, this should show how as you are further from the source you can hear less. This could be turned into a human graph and photographed.

- Play different sounds with students at different distances. Make the sounds and ask the students to take one pace further away until they cannot hear the sound any longer. Establish that sound decreases with distance and that different sounds can be heard over different distances.

- Make a listening map by sitting still (probably outdoors) and drawing sound sources with arrows to show where the sounds come from – short arrows for nearby sounds, longer arrows for those further away. Ensure a correct understanding of hearing by checking that the arrows point towards the hearer.

- Ask students to record a series of sounds, in order, increasing from the quietest to the loudest.

- Discuss situations which produce very loud sounds – aircraft, pneumatic drills, discos. *Why are they dangerous? What protective clothing can people wear?* Students can draw safety posters warning of the dangers of very loud sounds.

Differentiation

More able students can discuss why shouting louder doesn't always mean you get your own way! *Why do babies cry? How can we reason with others as we get older?* Discuss the dangers of hoax emergency calls.

Did you know?

The low pitched rumble or grumble that an elephant makes can be heard over 10 km away and is one of the ways that elephants communicate in the plains of Africa. A lion's roar can be heard almost as far away.

Dig deeper

Sounds travel well under water. You can test this at the swimming pool by banging a saucepan under water. All students under the water would hear it clearly.

I wonder...

Sound travels faster in liquids than in air and faster through solids than through liquids. This is to do with the particles that the sound travels through. The closer the particles are, the faster and further the sound can travel without losing energy. Particles are closest together in solids.

Other ideas

- Compare a range of ear protectors – use different absorbent materials strapped over ears with a large elastic band. *How can we make the comparison fair?* Use the same sound, distance, place and person.

- Consider silence. *When is it important to be quiet and why?* Can students read, listen to the television, or hear each other talking if there is a lot of other noise? Compare listening in quiet/silence to listening with distracting noise.

Presentation

WS 20

Use WS 20 to develop the use of descriptive language and sounds.

Students can write their own poem about sounds, focusing on them getting quieter as you go further away.

Plenary

- Conduct a class survey to find out their favourite and least favourite sounds. Ask the school staff, too. Is there a difference between students' and adults' preferences?

- *What sounds can you hear from further away?*

- Check that students know why loud sounds are dangerous. Can they relate this to how the ear works, touched on in the previous lesson? Ensure that the students know sounds come from different directions and spread out.

Unit 5: Sound – Diminishing distances

The objectives for this lesson are that students should be able to:

- Understand that sounds travel away from sources, getting fainter over longer distances

- Take part in a scientific investigation on how sound diminishes over distance

- Measure, collect and record information

- Record results in a chart or graph and share their findings.

SB pp.54–55 | Starter

- Ask students to suggest how you might hear better. *Will closing your eyes, cupping your ear or turning your head make a difference? Try it. Is hearing improved? Why?*

- Tell the scary story of *The Dark, Dark House* and ask students how they are sitting to ensure they hear you. (Any very quiet suspense story will work here.)

The challenge

Read page 54 of the *Student Book* and the argument going on between the two children. *What do they mean by "best"? Who do you think in the class would be best at hearing? Do they have the biggest ears? Do they have the shortest hair?*

What to do

In the hall, ask each student in turn to walk away from a tape recorder playing a quiet sound.

They should wave each time they hear the sound and stop when they can no longer hear it. Mark this spot. Measure the different distances with a trundle wheel and plot these on a bar chart. You can prevent cheating in this game by asking students to walk towards the sound. They must stop when they can hear it. You ask them what the sound is.

What you need

- Cones.

- A sound source.

- A trundle wheel.

- A digital camera for the recording of results.

What to check

Students may guess rather than concentrate on hearing the sound. Watch for evidence of significantly reduced hearing.

> ⚠️ Don't make sounds loud enough to damage the ear.

Differentiation

More able students should be able to interpret the bar chart and say what they show, creating their own charts with adult help.

What did you find?

Discuss the image shown in the *Student Book* on page 55. What does this show about the children listening to the sounds?

Record

What do students notice as they walk further away from a sound? Together, plot the loudness of sounds (using descriptions like 'very quiet') against distance on a bar chart. You could use road cones as listening points across the playground. Keeping the sound source constant makes the test fair.

Use a photograph of the cones or measure the distances and record these in a table. This can be transferred to a block graph.

Did you know?

Sound travels at 767 miles per hour, or over 1200 km per hour through air.

Plenary

- Can students decide where to stand in the playground to show where a sound would be loud or quiet in terms of distance from its source? Can they link the concepts loud and near, and quiet and far?

- Make the students into a 'Noisebusters' team. Ask them to listen around the school for unwanted noise and suggest ways of reducing it – carpets in the library, curtains in the dining hall, keeping doors closed, closing the windows facing a busy road – applying what they have learned about the source and transmission of sound.

New International Edition

Unit 5: Sound – Unit 5 Review

The objectives for this lesson are that students should be able to:

- Check what they have learned about sound in this Unit

- Find out how they are working towards, within and beyond the Grade 1 level.

SB p.56 ## Expectations

Note: *items in italic are this Unit's scientific enquiry expectations.*

At the end of this Unit students working towards Grade 1 level will:

- recognize and describe many sounds

- relate their sense of hearing to their ears

- *make and record observations of sounds*

- *make simple comparisons.*

In addition, students working within Grade 1 level will:

- describe how sounds are generated by specific objects

- state that they hear sounds through their ears

- describe what they observe when they move further away from a source of sound

- describe how sounds relate to animals or feelings

- *make observations or measurements relating to sounds*

- *try to answer questions about sound*

- *with help present these in charts.*

Further to this, students working beyond Grade 1 level will also:

- recognize that when sounds are generated by objects, something moves or vibrates

- *interpret data in simple charts.*

Check-up

This activity should allow the students to work on both distance and size of ears. Many of them will not automatically put the cups to their ears to listen!

You will need string and yoghurt pots, etc. of varying sizes.

Assessment

WS 21

Use the Unit 4 assessment to check the students' understanding of the content of the Unit. The answers are given opposite.

Name: _____ Date: _____

WS 21 **Unit 5 Assessment**

1 What sounds like this?

twang _____ bang _____

ping _____ tick _____

2 This is a xylophone. Write 'high' at the end of the xylophone that gives high notes. Write 'low' at the end that gives low notes.

_____   _____

3 Join the start and end of each sentence.

We hear sounds	in all directions.
Quick vibrations	with our ears.
Something has to move	make high notes.
Sound spreads out	to make a sound.

4 You cover your ears with your hands. What happens to sounds?

_____

_____

Why? _____

_____

Unit 5: Sound   21

Written assessment

Answers to WS 21, Unit 5 review

1 Accept appropriate answers.

2 High (left-hand); low (right-hand).

3 We hear sounds/with our ears.

   Big vibrations/make high notes.

   Something has to move/to make a sound.

   Sound spreads out/in all directions.

4 You are stopping/making it hard for sounds to reach your ears. Sounds are quieter. Any sound you make is just as loud!

For additional worksheets, either for fast workers or to review topics covered during the year, see worksheets 22 to 27.

The answer!

What if we lived on a planet without any words? How could we use sound to 'talk'? (See page 45, Student Book)

There are many ways to 'talk'. You can use sounds, to show how you feel, like animals do. You can use sign language to spell out words. You could use flags like they do on ships. Morse code is lots of beeps and was used by people before telephones were invented. The length of the beeps (dots and dashes) in Morse code, not their loudness or volume, is important. A 'dash' is a longer sound than a 'dot'. The dots and dashes translate to letters of the alphabet.

And finally...

Draw a large outline of a person and label all the sounds they can make with their body: clap with their hands, stamp with their feet, sing with their voice, etc.

Make a display of musical instruments, including ones from around the world. Mark their origins on a glove or on a map.

Write rhyming sounds and display them on the classroom wall along with any poetry or creative writing that the students have done.